WONDERFUL
WIRE
Works

An Easy Decorative Craft

WONDERFUL
WIRE
Works

Mickey Baskett

An Easy Decorative Craft

Sterling Publishing Co., Inc.
New York

Prolific Impressions Production Staff:

Editor: Mickey Baskett
Copy: Phyllis Mueller
Graphics: Dianne Miller, Prepress XPress
Photography: Skye Mason, Greg Wright
Administration: Jim Baskett
Styling: Laney Crisp McClure

Acknowledgements

Mickey Baskett thanks the following for their generous contributions:

The artists who contributed their talent to this book. These individuals have been generous enough to share their talent and knowledge of designing with wire. The following talented people made this book possible: Marion Brizendine, Beth Cosner, Patty Cox, Sonny Knox, Vivian Peritts.

For wire supplies:
Nasco Arts Crafts, 901 Janesville Avenue, P.O. Box 901, Fort Atkinson, WI 53538. 920-563-2446.

Every effort has been made to insure that the information presented is accurate. Since we have no control over physical conditions, individual skills, or chosen tools and products, the publisher disclaims any liability for injuries, losses, untoward results, or any other damages which may result from the use of the information in this book. Thoroughly read the instructions for all products used to complete the projects in this book, paying particular attention to all cautions and warnings shown for that product to ensure their proper and safe use.

Library of Congress Cataloging-in-Publication Data Available

Published in paperback in 2007 by Sterling Publishing Company, Inc.
387 Park Avenue South, New York, N.Y. 10016
Produced by Prolific Impressions, Inc.
160 South Candler St., Decatur, GA 30030
© 1999 by Prolific Impressions, Inc.
Distributed in Canada by Sterling Publishing
c/o Canadian Manda Group, 165 Dufferin Street
Toronto, Ontario, Canada M6K 3H6
Distributed in the United Kingdom by GMC Distribution Services
Castle Place, 166 High Street, Lewes, East Sussex, England BN7 1XU
Distributed in Australia by Capricorn Link (Australia) Pty. Ltd.
P.O. Box 704, Windsor, NSW 2756, Australia

Printed in Hong Kong
All rights reserved

Sterling ISBN-13: 978-0-8069-3943-8 Hardcover
        ISBN-10: 0-8069-3943-5
        ISBN-13: 978-1-4027-4406-8 Paperback
        ISBN-10: 1-4027-4406-4

For information about customs editions, special sales, or premium and corporate purchases, please contact Sterling Special Sales Department at 800-805-5489 or specialsales@sterlingpub.com.

Contents

Foreword
6

About Wire
8

Tools & Equipment
10

General Instructions
12

Making Wire Jewelry
14 - 43

Bottles & Vases
44 - 51

Tabletop Glamour
52 - 69

Lamps & Shades
70 - 79

Frames
80 - 99

Baskets
100 -105

Candle Holders
106 - 126

Metric Conversion Chart
127

Index
128

Foreword

Welcome to the wonderful ways wire can work for you—for jewelry, for decorating, for gift giving. The projects in this book showcase the versatility of wire. They are made from readily available supplies and are created by simply bending, wrapping, and forming the wire—no soldering is required!

Using just a few basic tools, you can create distinctive jewelry, terrific accessories for your table, a dazzling array of candle holders, frames, lampshades and lamp bases, and all sorts of interesting containers, including baskets, bud vases, and bottles. Step-by-step instructions, numerous illustrations, and complete patterns are provided.

From the project photos, you can see the variety of colors and differences in texture and sheen—shiny golds and silvers, gleaming coppers, glowing brass and bronze, the matte looks of aluminum and steel. Also evident is wire's ability to adapt to a wide variety of styles—fancy or funky, formal and informal, traditional or modern.

Wire is inexpensive to buy and so easy to form and manipulate. You're going to love working with wire. Enjoy! ∾

Mickey Baskett

About Wire

Wire is the generic name given to pliable metallic strands that are made in a variety of thicknesses and lengths. Two basic characteristics distinguish one kind of wire from another: the type of metal used and the thickness, usually referred to as the gauge or diameter. The higher the number of the gauge, the thinner the wire; e.g., 24 gauge wire is thinner than 16 gauge wire. The "Supplies" sections of the projects in this book list the type of metal and the thickness or gauge used.

The type of metal a wire is made of gives the wire its color, and wire is often referred to by the names of three metallic "colors"—gold, silver, and copper. **Gold-colored wire** *can be made of gold, brass, or bronze.* **Silver-colored wire** *can be made of silver, steel, aluminum, or tin-coated copper.* **Copper-colored wire** *is made of copper or copper plus another metal. The color of wire can be altered with spray paint, acrylic craft paint, or rub-on metallic wax. Wire also can be purchased in colors.*

Commercially, wire is used to impart structure and conduct electricity, so it's not surprising that it's sold in hardware and building supply stores and electrical supply houses.

You'll also find wire for sale in art supply stores, in crafts stores, and in stores that sell supplies for jewelry making, and from mail order catalogs.

Wire Types Used In Projects

Most any type of wire will work for the projects in this book. Just be sure to use the thickness of wire listed in the supplies to get the same results as shown. It is best to use a wire that is non-corrosive so that your projects will have a long life. All of the wire types listed are very pliable and easy to work with. Use any of the following wire types for the projects in this book.

Armature wire: A non-corrosive aluminum alloy wire, armature wire is easy to bend and doesn't tarnish. It is used by clay sculptors to build their armatures—the wire framework sculptures are built on. It is usually 1/8" or 1/4" thick or can be found by gauge measurement. You'll find it in stores that sell art and craft supplies. This is the wire that is used most for the projects in this book.

Buss wire: Buss wire is tin-coated copper wire used as an uninsulated conductor of electricity. Shinier than aluminum wire and inexpensive, buss wire is silver in color and often used for making jewelry. It's available in various gauges. Look for it at hardware stores and electrical supply houses.

Aluminum wire: Soft and flexible, aluminum wire is silver in color and has a dull finish. It won't rust and is often used for con-

structing electric fences. It's available at building supply and hardware stores.

Solder wire: Used by plumbers to solder pipe, solder wire is soft, silver-colored, and easy to bend. It comes on a spool and is sold by the pound. Be sure to buy solder that is solid core and lead-free. It can be found at hardware and building supply stores.

Thinner gauge wire: Bought by the spool or the package, thinner wire—from 16 to 28 gauge—can be made of a variety of metals, including sterling silver, brass, gold, copper, steel, and galvanized tin. You can find it in hobby shops, crafts stores, hardware stores, and stores that sell supplies for jewelry making.

Wire mesh: Used for window screens and filters and also called "wire cloth," wire mesh is available in brass, bronze, copper, and the more common aluminum. It comes on rolls that are 36" wide and it is sold by the foot. The number of the mesh (40 mesh, 100 mesh) denotes the number of holes per inch. Wire mesh with higher numbers is finer—almost like fabric—and is made of thinner wire. You'll find it at hardware stores; you also can check the telephone directory listing for "wire cloth." ∽

Pictured clockwise from top right: 1/4" armature wire, 1/8" armature wire, 19 gauge wire, 24 gauge galvanized wire, 16 gauge brass wire, solder wire, #40 wire mesh.

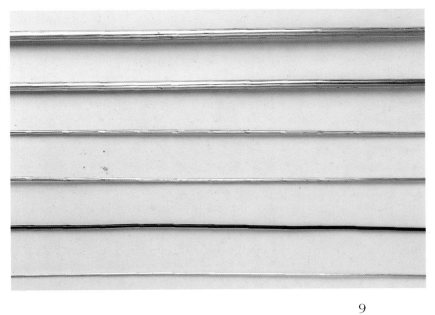

Various wires used are shown actual size at left. From top to bottom: 1/8" armature wire, 16 oz. solder wire, 16 gauge buss wire, 16 gauge brass wire, 19 gauge black wire, 24 gauge galvanized wire.

9

Tools & Equipment

Pliers

Pliers are used for bending, twisting, looping, and coiling wire.

Jewelry making pliers are the best type to use when working with delicate projects and materials.

Round nose pliers have rounded ends. Use smaller ones for delicate work and larger ones to make bigger loops.

Needle nose pliers or flat nose fliers, also called "snipe nose pliers," have flat inner surfaces and pointed ends.

Cutters

Available in a wide range of sizes, wire cutters are tools used for cutting wire. Thicker, lower gauge wire requires sturdy cutters. Very thin wire can be cut with smaller jewelry-making wire cutters. Very thin wire can be cut with **scissors** or **nail clippers** but it will dull these tools. Use **old scissors or metal shears** for cutting wire mesh.

Often pliers have a sharp edge that can be used for cutting wire. Use a **small file** for smoothing cut edges of wire or any rough spots.

Supplies for Making Templates

For some projects, instructions are given for creating templates from wood and dowels or nails for forming the wire. To make a template, you'll need:

Tracing paper for tracing the pattern for the template.
Transfer paper and a stylus for transferring the pattern.
Piece of wood for the template surface.
Small headless nails (3/4" wire brads work well in most cases) of small diameter.
Dowels for forming the wire. If you make a template using dowels, you'll also need a drill with a drill bit to make the holes for the dowels.

Glues

Several types of glue are used in wire projects. When using glues, be cautious! Many glues emit fumes as they dry. Always read the label and follow manufacturer's precautions and instructions. Work in a ventilated area and avoid contact with your skin.

Jewelry glue is a clear-drying glue made specifically for gluing metal and stones. Find it at crafts stores and stores that sell jewelry-making supplies.

Metal glue is just that—a glue that's meant to adhere metal to metal. Find it at crafts and hardware stores.

Household cement is a general purpose cement sold under a variety of trade names. It can be used for metal, china, glass, and paper. It's available at crafts and hardware stores.

Epoxy comes in two containers—one contains a resin, the other a hardener. When mixed, their chemical action creates a strong, clear bond. You'll find epoxy at crafts and hardware stores.

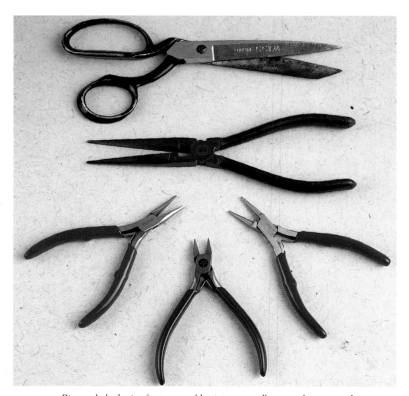

Pictured clockwise from top: old scissors, needle nose pliers, round nose jewelry pliers, wire cutters, flat nose jewelry pliers.

Pictured clockwise from top right: natural bone beads, metal beads, glass cabochons, glass beads - frosted and clear.

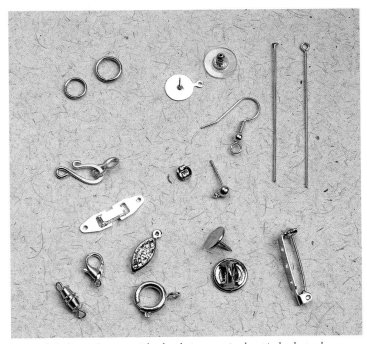

Pictured clockwise from top right: head pin, eye pin, bar pin back, push pin back, various clasps, two sizes of jump rings, pierced earring posts and backs.

Beads and Stones

Beads are made all over the world and can be found at crafts stores and the notions departments of variety and department stores. There are literally hundreds of shapes, sizes, and colors from which to choose. Beads are made of a variety of materials, including glass, wood, ceramic, metal, acrylic, semi-precious stones, and natural minerals. They are classified according to material, shape, and size. Beads have holes in them for stringing or threading on wire.

Stones don't have holes for stringing or threading, so when used with wire, they are wrapped with wire or glued in place. They may be of glass, natural minerals, acrylic, or semi-precious stones.

Cabochons are stones that are flat on one side, making them ideal for decorating flat surfaces.

Jewelry Findings

Findings are the metal items that transform wire and beads into jewelry. You will need the following:

Clasps: These come in a wide variety of shapes, sizes, and designs, Choose the type you like the best. You will find *barrel clasps, spring lock clasps,* and *fish hook/box clasps.*

Jump rings are small metal rings that are used to attach one finding to another such as to attach an eye pin to an earring back. They are split so that they can be pried open and shut for use.

Earring Backs come in both pierced and unpierced varieties. Pierced backs fall into two categories: *hooks* and *posts.* Unpierced backs are available in *screw-on* and *clip-on.*

Stick pins and pin backs are attached to your jewelry design to transform it into a pin.

Headpins are earring findings used to construct drop earrings. They come in a variety of lengths. Beads are threaded onto the pin then attached to an earring back. The head pin looks like a straight pin without a point at the tip.

Eyepins have a loop on the end and are used in the same manner as headpins.

Protective Gear

Wire can be sharp at the ends and could cause injury if caution is not used. For safety, wear **goggles** when nipping wire and **protective gloves** such as cotton or leather gardening gloves. ∽

General Instructions

The following techniques are used in some, not all, of the projects. Most of the projects merely require that you bend and shape the wire.

Making a Perfectly Symmetrical Twist

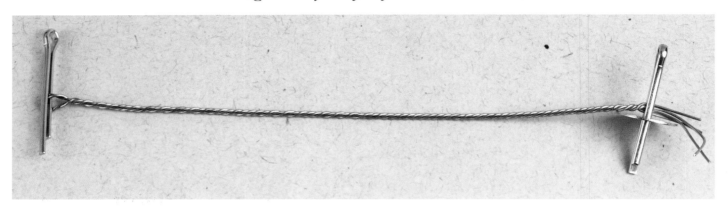

◆ YOU'LL NEED:

2 cotter pins, 2" x 3/16"
1 fender washer, 1-1/4" x 3/16"
2 pieces 16 gauge wire, each 24" long

◆ HERE'S HOW:

1. Thread the wires through the eye of one cotter pin and fold wires in half at center around cotter pin. (Fig. 1)
2. Slide the cut ends between the arms of a second cotter pin. Hold ends of wires flat in cotter pin. Tighten the hold by sliding a fender washer on the end of the second cotter pin. (Fig. 1)
3. Slide folded ends down between arms of first cotter pin. (Fig. 2)
4. Holding a cotter pin in each hand, twist one pin toward you while twisting the other pin away from you to make a rope-like strand. (Fig. 2)
5. Remove pins from twisted wire. ∾

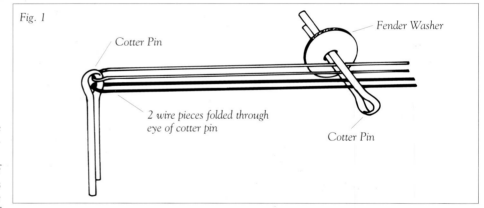

Fig. 1

Cotter Pin

Fender Washer

2 wire pieces folded through eye of cotter pin

Cotter Pin

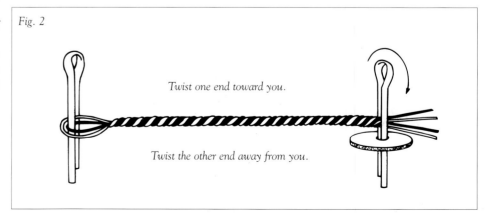

Fig. 2

Twist one end toward you.

Twist the other end away from you.

Constructing a Flat Coil Maker

◆ YOU'LL NEED:

1 threaded bolt, 2" x 3/16"
3 nuts, 3/16"
2 fender washers, 1-1/4" x 3/16"
16 gauge wire
File
Needle nose pliers

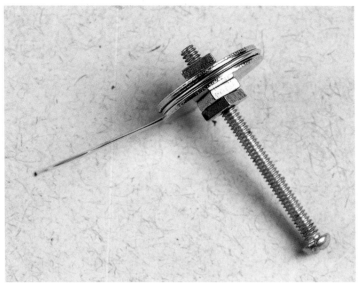

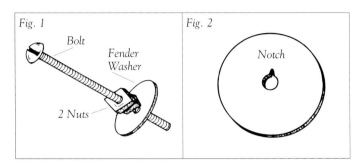

Fig. 1 — Bolt, Fender Washer, 2 Nuts
Fig. 2 — Notch

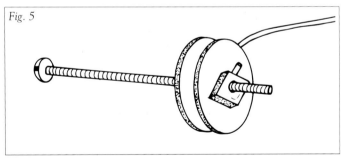

Fig. 3
Fig. 4

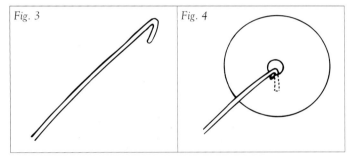

Fig. 5

◆ HERE'S HOW:

1. Screw two nuts on bolt about 3/4" from threaded end. Add one fender washer. (Fig. 1)
2. File a small notch on inside opening of other fender washer. (Fig. 2)
3. Make a 30 degree bend in wire 3/16" from the end. (Fig. 3)
4. Hook bend in wire in notch of fender washer. (Fig. 4)
5. Slide notched fender washer on bolt next to first fender washer, with the wire length between the washers. The bent tip of the wire should be on outside of washers. Screw remaining nut tightly against second washer. (Fig. 5)
6. Hold stem of bolt in fingers of one hand with thumb on top of fender washer near the threaded end. Hold length of wire in other hand. Turn bolt to form a flat coil of wire between the washers. Press top of washer with thumb while turning to open coiling side of washers. (Fig. 6)
7. When wire coil reaches desired size or the edge of the washer, unscrew bolt from end. Remove washer and coil from bolt.
8. Trim starting bend in wire with cutting edge of needle nose pliers. ∾

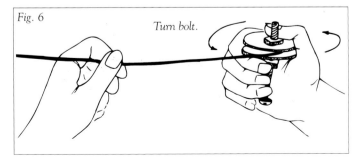

Fig. 6 — Turn bolt.

Making Wire Jewelry

It's easy to make great looking necklaces, earrings, bracelets, pendants, and pins—all from easy-to-manipulate WIRE! Using ordinary wire that can be found in hardware stores and art supply and craft shops—teamed with an assortment of beads, stones, and jewelry findings, you can create a variety of jazzy costume jewelry looks. All the tools you need are wire snips and needle-nose pliers—no soldering required!

Some of the items you can create are a chunky necklace of gold-wrapped amber beads, a delicate multi-strand mother-of-pearl choker, a sophisticated bracelet of copper coils, fun pins to enliven a lapel or a simple dress, and many, many more. You'll be amazed at the ease of making these exciting pieces. AND, think how much you'll enjoy wearing jewelry creations you made yourself!

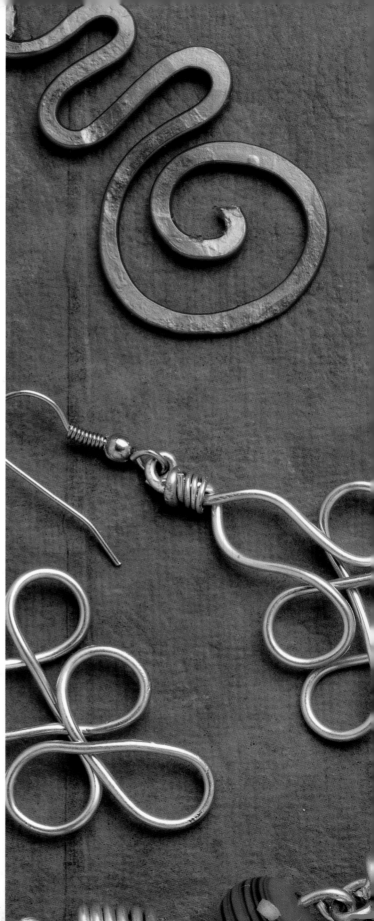

Wrapped Amber

NECKLACE & EARRINGS

Designed by Patty Cox

Length:
Necklace - 21"
Earring - 3/4" (excluding finding)

◆ SUPPLIES

20 gauge gold wire
13 round 10mm amber-colored beads
10 larger irregularly shaped amber-colored
    beads (sizes vary from approximately
    18mm to 25mm)
Gold necklace clasp
22 gold jump rings
2 gold French hook earring findings

◆ TOOLS

Round nose pliers
Needle nose pliers

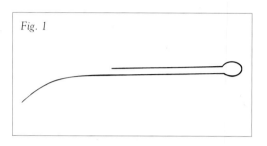

Fig. 1

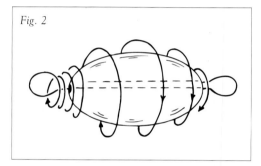

Fig. 2

◆ INSTRUCTIONS

Wrapping the Beads:
1. Cut a 12" length of gold wire. Hold wire 1" away from end with round nose pliers. Fold wire in half over round nose, forming a loop. (Fig. 1)
2. Add a bead over both wires. Form a wire loop on other end of bead. Wrap wire loop on other end of bead. Wrap wire tightly around loop. Continue spiraling wire around bead. End wire tightly around other loop. (Fig. 2) Repeat for each bead.

Assembling the Earrings:
3. Wrap two round beads for earrings, 1 for each earring.
4. Attach one wrapped round bead to each earring finding.

Assembling the Necklace:
5. Wrap 11 round beads and 10 larger beads for necklace.
6. Attach 11 wrapped round beads and 10 larger wrapped beads together with jump rings, starting with a wrapped round bead and alternating round and larger beads.
7. Attach necklace clasp at ends with jump rings. ∽

Gold Spirals & Green Beads

NECKLACE & EARRINGS

Designed by Patty Cox

Length:
Necklace - 21-1/2"
Earring - 2" (excluding finding)

◆ **SUPPLIES**

20 gauge gold wire
12 green glass beads, 18 mm
15 green glass beads, 8 mm
Gold necklace clasp
26 gold jump rings
2 gold French hook earring findings

◆ **TOOLS**

Round nose pliers
Needle nose pliers
Nail clippers

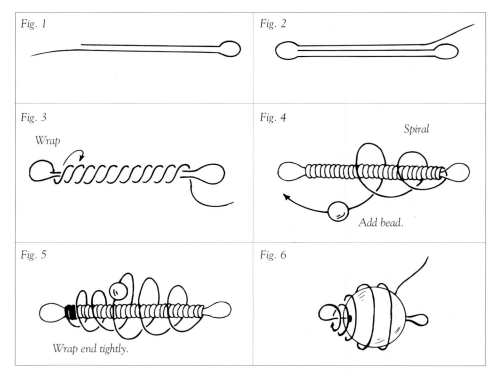

Fig. 1

Fig. 2

Fig. 3
Wrap

Fig. 4
Spiral
Add bead.

Fig. 5
Wrap end tightly.

Fig. 6

◆ **INSTRUCTIONS**

Making Wrapped Wire Spiral Beads:
1. Cut a 16" length of gold wire. Fold wire end back 3/4" over round nose pliers, forming a loop. (Fig. 1) Grasp wire 1" from loop with round nose pliers. Form a loop around round nose pliers. (Fig. 2)
2. Tightly wrap the wire shaft between the loops. (Fig. 3)
3. Loosely wrap a spiral around shaft, adding an 8 mm glass bead on the spiral. (Fig. 4) Wrap end tightly at loop. (Fig. 5) Clip excess wire with nail clippers. Make 11 spiral beads for necklace. Make two for earrings.

Wrapping the Round Beads:
4. Cut a 6" length of gold wire. Hold wire 1" away from end with round nose pliers. Fold wire in half over round nose, forming a loop. (Fig. 1)
5. Add an 18 mm bead over both wires. Form a wire loop on other end of bead. Wrap wire loop on other end of bead. Wrap wire tightly around loop. Continue spiraling wire around bead. End wire tightly around other loop. (Fig. 6) Wrap 10 beads for necklace. Wrap two for earrings.

Assembling the Earrings:
6. Attach a spiral bead to a wrapped bead with a jump ring. Repeat for other earring.
7. Attach end with wrapped wire spiral bead to each earring finding.
8. Thread an 8 mm bead on a jump ring. Attach at end of wrapped round bead. Repeat for other earring.

Assembling the Necklace:
9. Attach 11 wrapped wire spiral beads and 10 wrapped round beads together with jump rings, starting with a spiral bead and alternating spiral and round beads.
10. Attach necklace clasp at ends with jump rings. ∽

Mother of Pearl Nuggets

CHOKER & EARRINGS

Designed by Patty Cox

Length:
Necklace - 16"
Earring - 2" (excluding findings)

♦ **SUPPLIES**

24 gauge gold wire
Mother of pearl nuggets with beading
   holes, about 180 pieces
19 gold beads, 7 mm
64 gold seed beads
Gold necklace clasp
4 gold jump rings
2 gold French hook earring findings

♦ **TOOLS**

Round nose pliers
Needle nose pliers
Nail clippers

♦ **INSTRUCTIONS**

The choker and earrings are made of sections that are constructed of beads and wire. The technique is the same for each section, but the composition varies. (See Figs. 1 - 4 for supplies used in each section.) You'll need to make five strands: three strands of three-nugget sections (two strands with 13 sections and one strand with 15 sections), one strand with nine five-nugget sections and three gold bead sections, and one strand with 16 gold bead sections.

Making One Section:

1. Cut a 5-6" length of gold wire. Hold wire 1/2" away from end with round nose pliers. Fold wire in half over round nose, forming a loop.
2. Wrap wire tightly around loop. Wrap wire shaft about 3/16". Add seed beads

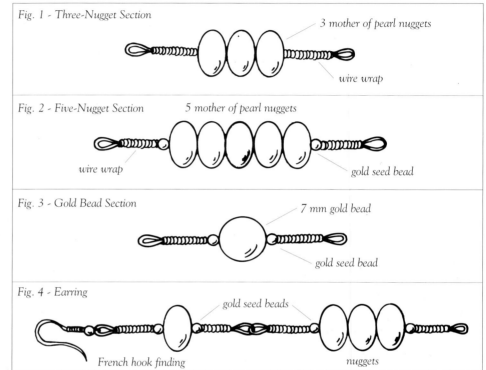

Fig. 1 - Three-Nugget Section — 3 mother of pearl nuggets — wire wrap

Fig. 2 - Five-Nugget Section — 5 mother of pearl nuggets — wire wrap — gold seed bead

Fig. 3 - Gold Bead Section — 7 mm gold bead — gold seed bead

Fig. 4 - Earring — gold seed beads — French hook finding — nuggets

and/or nuggets and/or gold bead, depending on which section you're making. Fold ending wire 3/8" from nuggets or beads. Form a loop over round nose pliers. Wrap wire tightly around loop. Wrap wire shaft. Clip end of wire with nail clippers.

Assembling the Necklace:

3. After completing one section, start the next one by looping the wire piece for the next section through the previous one. Continue to add sections until necklace strands are complete.
4. On each end, attach the five strands to one jump ring.
5. Add a second jump ring to each end.
6. Attach the clasp to the jump rings.

Assembling the Earrings:

7. For each earring, make one section with two gold seed beads and one mother of pearl nugget. Add to that one section with three mother of pearl nuggets and two gold seed beads. See Fig. 4.
8. Add a French hook finding to each earring. ∽

Copper Coils

BRACELET & EARRINGS

Designed by Patty Cox

Size:
Bracelet - 8" long, including clasp
Earring - 1" diameter

◆ SUPPLIES

16 gauge copper wire (8 ft. in all)
9 black cabochons, 18 mm
9 silver jump rings
Silver bracelet hook
2 flat pad ear posts, 19 mm
Jewelry glue

◆ TOOLS

Flat coil maker (see General Instructions)
Round nose pliers
Needle nose pliers

Fig. 1

end coil

Make two for earrings without end coil.
Make seven for bracelet.

◆ INSTRUCTIONS

Making the Bracelet:
1. Cut seven 10" lengths of copper wire. Make seven flat coils for bracelet, using Flat Coil Maker. Coil the 3/4" end wire on each coil with round nose pliers. (See Fig. 1)
2. Connect the seven coils with jump rings, attaching the small end coil of one flat coil to the outer ring of another flat coil.
3. Attach bracelet hook to outer ring of end flat coil with a jump ring.
4. Glue a cabochon in the center of each coil.

Making the Earrings:
5. Cut two 10" lengths of copper wire. Make two flat coils for earrings, using Flat Coil Maker. Tuck the end of the wire under the coil.
6. Glue a cabochon in the center of each earring.
7. Glue a flat pad ear post to the back of each earring. ෆ

Pictured left to right: Woven Basket
Pendant (instructions on page 24),
Copper Coil Bracelet and Earrings
(instructions on page 22).

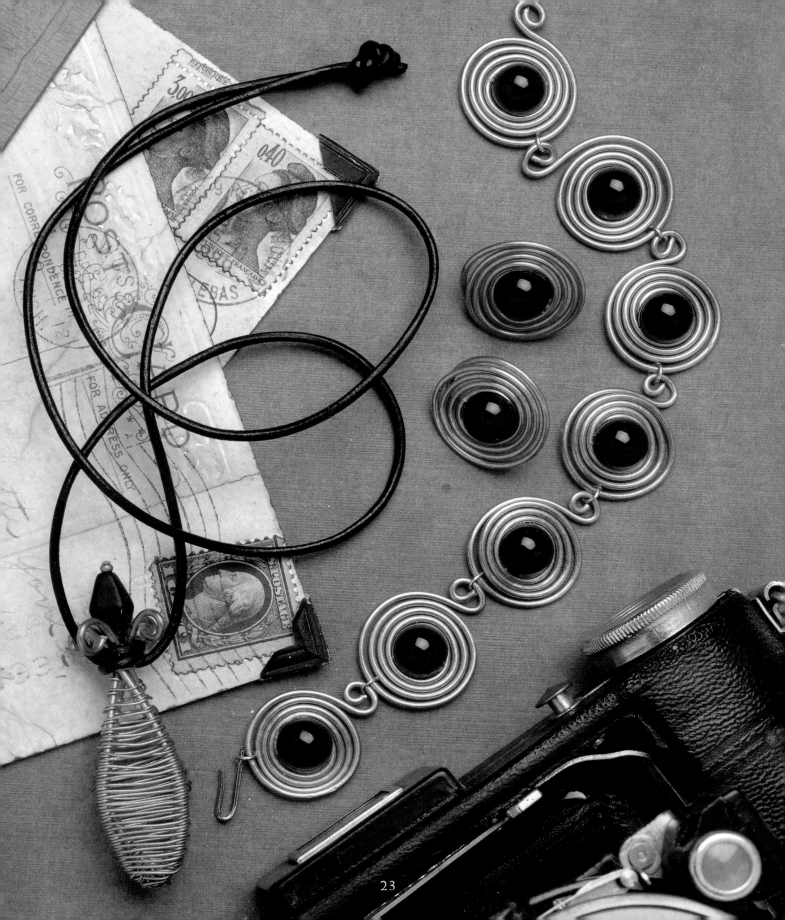

Woven Basket

PENDANT NECKLACE

Pictured on page 23

Designed by Patty Cox

Size - 2-1/2" long

◆ SUPPLIES

16 gauge copper wire
24 gauge copper wire
2 yds. black leather cording
Diamond shaped black bead, 1/2" long
Copper seed bead
Straight pin
Jewelry glue

◆ TOOLS

Round nose pliers
Scissors

◆ INSTRUCTIONS

1. Cut two 7" lengths of 16 gauge wire. Bend into base shape. See Fig. 1.
2. Align shapes next to each other. Wire neck of pendant together tightly with 24 gauge wire. (This will be removed after basket has been woven.)
3. Open base shapes, making four "spokes." Wire bottom points together at center of spokes with an "x" of 24 gauge wire.
4. Cut 2 yds. 24 gauge wire. Beginning at the bottom point (the x), wrap end of wire around bottom of one spoke three times.
5. Bring wire to next spoke. Wrap once. Pull wire tightly. Continue around the shape, wrapping the spokes, until you reach the top.
6. Remove temporary 24 gauge wire at neck. Wrap remaining weaving wire around neck of pendant.
7. Trim ends of spokes to 3/4". Roll each spoke into a small coil with round nose pliers.
8. Wrap center of leather cording twice around neck of pendant. Tie at back in an overhand knot. Bring leather ends together. Tie ends in an overhand knot. Trim ends with scissors.
9. Thread a copper seed bead and the black bead on a straight pin. Dot glue on base of black bead. Insert pin into top of pendant. ∾

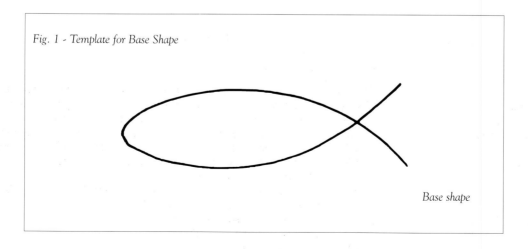

Fig. 1 - Template for Base Shape

Base shape

Golden Wrapping

BRACELET WITH CENTER WRAP

Pictured on page 27

Designed by Patty Cox

◆ SUPPLIES

16 gauge silver buss wire
22 gauge gold wire

◆ TOOLS

Wire cutters on needle nose pliers

◆ INSTRUCTIONS

1. Cut a 31" length of 16 gauge silver buss wire. Measure 5" and make a 1/2" rounded bend in wire. Measure 7" and make another bend. (Fig. 1) Make two rounds of wire, forming an oval 7" long with a 5" piece after the second bend. (Fig. 2)
2. Cut a 24" length of 22 gauge gold wire. Press silver wires in center of oval together tightly. Wrap gold wire around center, securing ends. When wrapping is complete, clips tails of silver and gold wires close to the wrapped center.
3. Bend wire around wrist to size the bracelet. Remove and fashion into a symmetrical shape. ∽

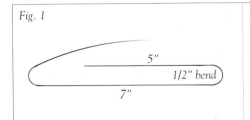

Fig. 1
5"
1/2" bend
7"

Fig. 2
Press silver wire at center.
Wrap center with gold wire.

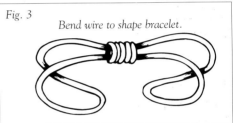

Fig. 3
Bend wire to shape bracelet.

Wire Twists

TWO BRACELETS

Pictured on page 27

Designed by Patty Cox

◆ SUPPLIES

For one bracelet:
13 gauge copper wire, 24" long
13 gauge silver buss wire, 24" long
2 silver or copper end caps

◆ TOOLS

2 cotter pins, 2" x 3/16"
1 fender washer, 1-1/4" x 3/16"
Wire cutters
Jewelry glue
Optional: Hammer and anvil or brick

◆ INSTRUCTIONS

The photo on page 27 shows two silver and copper bracelets, one twisted but not flattened, the other twisted and flattened. The two bracelets are made using the same basic technique. See "Making a Perfectly Symmetrical Twist" in the General Instructions.

1. Thread the silver and copper wires through the eye of one cotter pin and fold wire in half at center around cotter pin. Slide looped ends down between arms of cotter pin.
2. Slide the cut ends between the arms of a second cotter pin. Tighten the hold by sliding a fender washer on the end of the cotter pin.
3. Holding a cotter pin each hand, twist one pin toward you while twisting the other pin away from you to make a rope-like strand.
4. Remove pins from twisted wire. Wrap twisted wire around wrist and mark cutting lines. Cut at marks with wire cutters.
5. Glue end caps on cut ends.
6. *Optional:* To make flattened twist bracelet, place twisted wire on an anvil or a brick and pound flat with a hammer.
7. Form wire into an oval shape. ∽

Coils & Twists

PIN & EARRINGS

Designed by Patty Cox

◆ SUPPLIES

13 gauge copper wire
13 gauge silver buss wire
2 earring posts, 19 mm
Bar pin back, 1-1/2"
Thin piece of clear plexiglass, 1-5/8" x 3/8"

◆ TOOLS

2 cotter pins, 2" x 3/16"
1 fender washer, 1-1/4" x 3/16"
Wire cutters
Round nose pliers
Jewelry glue
Flat Coil Maker (see General
  Instructions)

◆ INSTRUCTIONS

Making the Twist:
See "Making a Perfectly Symmetrical Coil" in the General Instructions.

1. Cut two 24" pieces of copper wire. Cut two 24" pieces of silver wire. Thread the one piece of silver wire and one piece of copper wire through the eye of one cotter pin and fold wire in half at center around cotter pin. Slide looped ends down between arms of cotter pin.
2. Slide the cut ends between the arms of a second cotter pin. Tighten the hold by sliding a fender washer on the end of the cotter pin.
3. Holding a cotter pin each hand, twist one pin toward you while twisting the other pin away from you to make a symmetrical twist.
4. Remove pins from twisted wire.
5. Repeat with remaining two pieces of wire.

Making the Base Coils:
6. Cut two 10" pieces silver wire. Make

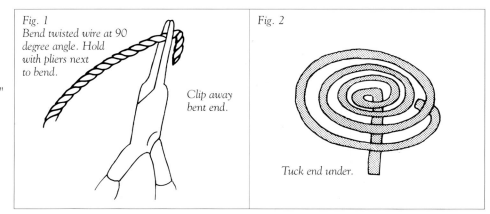

Fig. 1
Bend twisted wire at 90 degrees angle. Hold with pliers next to bend.

Clip away bent end.

Fig. 2

Tuck end under.

two flat coils for earrings 3/4" in diameter, using the Flat Coil Maker. Tuck the ends of the wire under the coils.

7. Cut two 5" pieces silver wire and one 12" piece silver wire. Make three flat coils for pin, two small (3/8" in diameter) and one large (1" in diameter), using the Flat Coil Maker. Tuck the ends of the wires under the coils.

Assembling the Earrings:
8. Cut one piece of twisted wire in half. Bend one end of one piece at a 90 degree angle 1/4" from end. Hold wire with round nose pliers next to the bend. (Fig. 1)
9. Coil twisted wire to make a disk 7/8" in diameter. Tuck end of twisted wire under coil. (Fig. 2) Lightly press center of coil outward, forming a slightly domed shape. Glue coiled silver and copper twisted wire on a 3/4" flat silver coil, placing the undersides of both pieces together.
10. Glue earring post to flat coil back.
11. Repeat for other earring.

Assembling the Pin:
12. Cut two pieces, each 2" long, from the second piece of twisted wire. (You now have three pieces—two 2" and one longer one.) Bend one end of one piece at a 90 degree angle 1/4" from end. Hold wire with round nose pliers next to the bend. (Fig. 1)
13. Coil twisted wire to make a disk. Tuck end of twisted wire under coil. (Fig. 2) Clip away bent end. Lightly press center of coil outward, forming a slightly domed shape.
14. Repeat with remaining two pieces of twisted wire to make two more coils. (You'll have three coils—one 1-1/8" in diameter and two 1/2" in diameter.)
15. Glue the 1/2" coiled silver and copper twisted wires on the 3/8" flat silver coils, placing the undersides of both pieces together.
16. Glue the 1-1/8" coiled silver and copper twisted wire on the 1" flat silver coils, placing the undersides of both pieces together.
17. Arrange the three coils, with the larger one in the center, on the clear plexiglass piece. Glue in place.
18. Glue bar pin back on back of plexiglass piece. ∽

Pictured clockwise from top: Coil Twists Pin & Earrings (instructions on page 26), Wire Twists Bracelets (instructions on page 25), Golden Wrapping Bracelet (instructions on page 25).

Red & Silver

NECKLACE WITH RED BEADS

Designed by Patty Cox

Length - 18", excluding clasp

♦ **SUPPLIES**

16 gauge silver buss wire
3 red glass beads, 28 mm
6 red glass beads, 18 mm
Silver necklace clasp

♦ **TOOLS**

Round nose pliers
Needle nose pliers

♦ **INSTRUCTIONS**

This necklace is made up of three types of units: large beads wrapped with wire, small beads with loops of wire on either end, and wrapped wire beads.

Wrapping the Large Beads:

1. For each bead, cut a 2" piece of wire. Slide wire through center of large bead. Using needle nose pliers, make a loop in each end of wire, leaving a 3/8" wire stem on each side of bead. (Fig. 1)
2. Cut a 16" piece of wire. Tightly wrap end of wire around one loop of wire stem on bead. Wrap wire around stem, gradually increasing size of wrap to size of bead. Make a spiral of wire around the bead, then wrap stem, gradually decreasing the size of the wrap, ending tightly around loop on other end of stem. (Fig. 2)
3. Repeat with remaining two large beads.

Hooking the Small Beads:

4. Cut a 3/4" piece of wire. Make a loop on one end. Add a small bead on wire. Make a loop on other end. (Fig. 3)
5. Repeat with remaining beads—six in all.

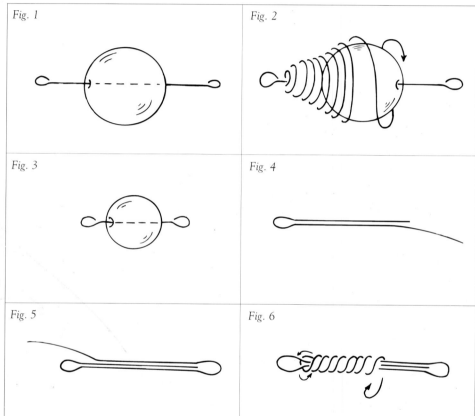

Fig. 1   Fig. 2   Fig. 3   Fig. 4   Fig. 5   Fig. 6

Making the Wrapped Wire Spirals:

6. For each piece, cut a 12" length of wire. Fold wire over round nose pliers 3/4" from one end. Use needle nose pliers to close loop. (Fig. 4)
7. Fold wire over round nose pliers 1" from first loop to make a second loop. (Fig. 5)
8. Holding the wire at the first loop with needle nose pliers, wrap the end of the wire around the three wires between the loops to make a spiral. (Fig. 6)
9. Repeat, making eight in all. Then make two more, but before closing the loops and wrapping, attach the spiral to one of the other spirals to make a pair of spirals for the ends.

Assembling the Necklace:

10. Working from one end, assemble the necklace by connecting the loops: two wire spirals, one small red bead, one wire spiral, one small red bead, one wire spiral, one large wrapped red bead, one wire spiral, one small red bead, one large wrapped bead. Repeat order in reverse to complete.
11. Attach clasp at ends. ∾

Pictured from top: Figure Eights Earrings (instructions on page 30), Red & Silver Necklace (instructions on page 28), Copper Swirls Earrings (instructions on page 30).

Figure Eights

SILVER EARRINGS

Pictured on page 29

Designed by Patty Cox

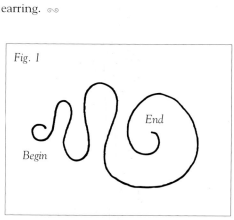

Fig. 1
Jig Pattern

Begin
bottom

top

Length - 2-1/8" long, excluding ear wire

◆ SUPPLIES

16 gauge silver buss wire
24 gauge silver wire
2 French hook earring wires

◆ TOOLS & EQUIPMENT

Round nose pliers
For the template:
1/4" diameter dowel, 8" long
Saw
6" piece of 2 x 4 lumber
Drill and 1/4" bit
Tracing paper
Transfer paper and stylus

◆ INSTRUCTIONS

Making the Template:
1. Trace pattern for template. (Fig. 1)
   Transfer pattern to 2 x 4 wood.
2. Drill holes 3/8" deep in 2 x 4.
3. Cut dowel in pieces 1" long. Insert dowel pieces in holes.

Making the Earrings:
4. Cut two pieces of 16 gauge wire, each 18" long. Cut two pieces of 24 gauge wire, six 6" long.
5. Find center of one piece of 16 gauge wire. Fold wire at center around end dowel on template. (Fig. 1) Pull wire ends to center, criss cross, and wrap around next two dowels. Continue wrapping in a figure eight, ending wires around other end dowel. Twist wires once around end dowel. (This end is the top of the earring.) Lift wire from template.
6. Wrap top of earring at top twist with one piece of 24 gauge wire.
7. Trim tails of 16 gauge wire to 1/2". Grasp the end of one 1/2" tail with round nose pliers. Twist into a closed circle. Wrap other tail around neck of earring.
8. Make other earring, repeating steps 5 - 7.
9. Attach a French hook at the top of each earring. ∾

Copper Swirls

DANGLE EARRINGS

Pictured on page 29

Designed by Patty Cox

Length - 2" long, excluding finding

◆ SUPPLIES

16 gauge copper wire
2 gold jump rings
2 gold French hook earring findings

◆ TOOLS & EQUIPMENT

Hammer   Anvil or brick
Needle nose pliers   Round nose pliers

◆ INSTRUCTIONS

1. Cut two 5" lengths 16 gauge wire.
2. Hold end of one piece of wire with needle nose pliers and form a swirl, using Fig. 1 as a pattern. Shape the curves, ending with a tight swirl shaped on round nose pliers.
3. With second piece of wire, make a second swirl like the first.
4. Place wires on anvil or brick. Pound flat with a hammer.
5. Close top swirl of each tightly with needle nose pliers. Add a jump ring in each closed swirl.
6. Attach French hooks in each jump ring. ∾

Fig. 1

End

Begin

Cobalt & Copper

BEADED BRACELET

Pictured on page 33

Designed by Patty Cox

Fig. 1

ends

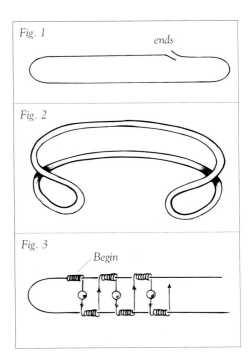

Fig. 2

Fig. 3

Begin

◆ **SUPPLIES**

10 gauge copper wire
24 gauge copper wire
14 cobalt blue glass beads, 1/8" diameter

◆ **TOOLS**

Needle nose pliers

◆ **INSTRUCTIONS**

1. Cut a 20" length of 10 gauge wire. Taper each end with a diagonal cut. Shape wire into an oval, overlapping cut ends. (Fig. 1)
2. Wrap tapered cut ends together with 24 gauge wire. Secure ends of wire. Clip tails.
3. Bend oval to fit wrist. (Fig. 2)
4. Cut a length of 24 gauge wire about 20" long. Using Fig. 3 as a guide, wrap wire around upper wire of bracelet five times. Add a blue bead. Wrap wire around lower wire of bracelet five times. Bring wire to upper bracelet wire and wrap five times. Continue wrapping this way, adding a bead every other wrap. To begin or end a length of wire, slide tail under five wraps. Pull tight with needle nose pliers. Cut wire close to wraps. ∾

Mardi Gras

DANGLE BEAD EARRINGS

Pictured on page 33

Designed by Beth Cosner

Fig. 1

Fig. 2

Fig. 3

Back of bead

Fig. 4

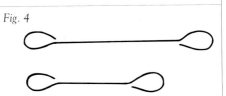

Length - 2-1/2"

◆ **SUPPLIES**

6 pearl pony beads, 9 mm (2 green, 2 blue, 2 turquoise)
Lead free solid plumbing solder, .081 gauge
2 silver earring posts

◆ **TOOLS & EQUIPMENT**

Block of wood 3/4" thick
5/64" drill bit
Drill
Wire cutters
Round nose pliers
Needle nose pliers
Jewelry glue

◆ **INSTRUCTIONS**

Making the Wired Beads:
1. Drill a hole through the wood block with a 5/64" drill bit.
2. Cut six pieces of wire, each 3-3/4" long.
3. Make a loop on one end of one piece of wire. (Fig. 1)
4. Thread the wire through the hole in the block of wood. Slide one bead on the wire. Bend the wire around the bead, ending with a loop. (Fig. 2)
5. Cut off the loop from the other side of the block of wood and remove the wired bead.
6. Bend the remaining wire into a swirl on the back of the bead. (Fig. 3)
7. Repeat steps 3 - 6 with remaining five beads.

Assembling the Earrings:
8. Cut two pieces of wire, each 1-1/2" long. Cut two more pieces of wire, each 2" long. Form a loop on each end of each piece to make the dangles. (Fig. 4)
9. Attach a blue wired bead to each 2" dangle. Attach a turquoise bead to each 1-1/2" dangle.
10. Attach one dangling blue bead and one dangling turquoise bead to each green bead.
11. Glue the posts on the backs of the green wired beads. ∾

Dappled with Gold

BRACELET

Designed by Beth Cosner

Length - 8-3/4", excluding clasp

◆ SUPPLIES

10 unfinished round wooden beads, 14 mm
Acrylic craft paint, copper metallic
Gold foil
Gold leaf adhesive
Gold leaf sealer
Lead-free plumbing solder, .081 gauge
16 gauge brass wire
6 gold split jump rings
1 gold lobster claw clasp, 14 mm

◆ TOOLS & EQUIPMENT

1/2" diameter dowel
1/16" diameter dowel, 12" long
Craft paint brushes
Wire cutters
Round nose pliers
Needle nose pliers
Small paint brushes

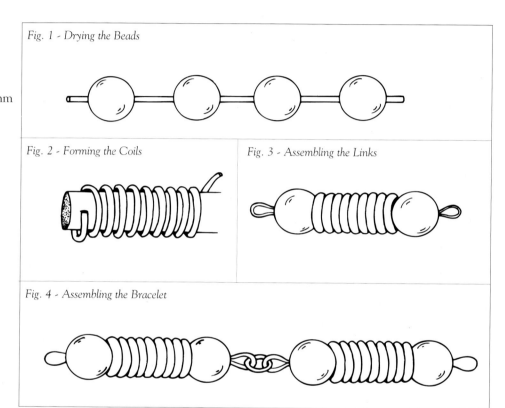

Fig. 1 - Drying the Beads

Fig. 2 - Forming the Coils

Fig. 3 - Assembling the Links

Fig. 4 - Assembling the Bracelet

◆ INSTRUCTIONS

Painting the Beads:

1. Paint the 10 beads with copper paint. Let dry. Apply a second coat. Let dry overnight. *Tip: Place the beads on a 1/16" dowel to dry.* (Fig. 1)
2. Dab gold leaf adhesive on the painted beads, but don't cover the copper paint completely. (The adhesive will become clear and tacky in 30 minutes to an hour.)
3. Press gold foil on the beads over the adhesive. Some of the copper paint will show through the gold.
4. Brush beads with gold leaf sealer. Let dry overnight.

Forming the Coils:

5. Tightly wrap plumbing solder around the 1/2" dowel until you have a coil 3/4" long (nine wraps). (Fig. 2) Snip the solder at each end with wire cutters. Slip coil off dowel.
6. Repeat to make five coils in all.

Assembling the Links:

7. Form a loop at one end of 16 gauge brass wire with round nose pliers.
8. Thread on one wooden bead, one coil, and one wooden bead.
9. Snip off the wire, leaving enough to make a loop at the other end. Make the loop. (Fig. 3)
10. Repeat to make five links in all.

Assembling the Bracelet:

11. Join the five links with four jump rings.
12. Attach a jump ring at each end.
13. Attach the clasp at one end. ∾

Pictured from top: Mardi Gras Earrings (instructions on page 31), Cobalt & Copper Bracelet (instructions on page 31), Dappled with Gold Bracelet (instructions on page 32).

Silver Spider

PIN

Designed by Marion Brizendine

Length - 3"

◆ SUPPLIES

16 gauge silver wire
22 gauge copper wire
Round copper bead, 12 mm
Flat copper bead, 4 mm x 12 mm in diameter
Teardrop copper bead, 1-1/4" long

◆ TOOLS

Needle nose pliers
Round nose pliers

◆ INSTRUCTIONS

1. Cut one piece of silver wire 4-1/2" long. Cut another piece 2-1/4" long. Make loops on the ends to form the antennae. Twist them together and twist the shorter wire around the longer wire.
2. Thread on the round copper bead and the flat copper bead over the twisted wire.
3. Cut 4 pieces of wire, each 4" long, for the legs. Bend each piece to form a half circle.
4. Place legs below beads across wire stem. Cut a 2" piece of copper wire. Wrap in and around centers of leg pieces. Coil the end to secure.
5. Thread teardrop-shaped bead on stem. Loop end to secure bead. ∾

Pictured from top: Sweet Rose Pin (instructions on page 37), Silver Butterfly Stick Pin (instructions on page 37), Copper Cat, Silver & Copper Cat (instructions on page 36).

Copper Cat

STICK PIN

Pictured on page 35

Designed by Patty Cox

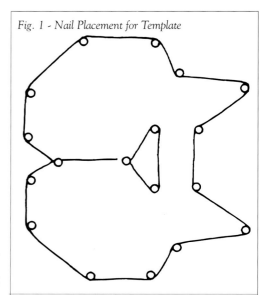

Fig. 1 - Nail Placement for Template

◆ **SUPPLIES**

16 gauge copper wire
24 gauge copper wire
2 oval black beads, 8 mm
Stick pin

◆ **TOOLS & EQUIPMENT**

Needle nose pliers
Jewelry glue
18 small headless nails
Wooden board
Hammer
Tracing paper
Transfer paper and stylus
Large straight pin

◆ **INSTRUCTIONS**

Making the Template:
1. Trace pattern for template. Transfer to board.
2. Hammer nails at markings. (Fig. 1)

Forming the Wire:
3. Cut a 12" piece of 16 gauge wire. Add black beads to wire.
4. Bend wire in shape of template, beginning and ending in the muzzle area. (Fig. 2)
5. Cut two 12" pieces of 24 gauge wire. Form whiskers from one piece of wire according to pattern in Fig. 3, twisting each whisker as it is formed. To twist a whisker, insert a large straight pin through looped end and turn.
6. Place whiskers at center of muzzle. Wrap whiskers on muzzle with remaining piece of 24 gauge wire to attach.
7. Bend each whisker in a zigzag. Round each whisker forward.
8. Glue pin on back. ∾

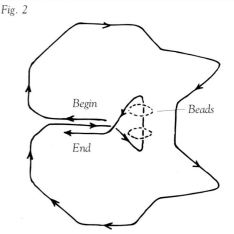

Fig. 2

Begin

Beads

End

Silver & Copper Cat

STICK PIN

Pictured on page 35

Designed by Patty Cox

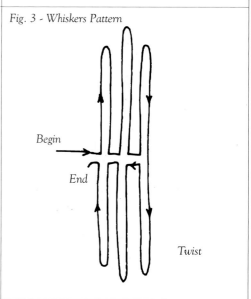

Fig. 3 - Whiskers Pattern

Begin

End

Twist

◆ **SUPPLIES**

16 gauge copper wire
24 gauge silver wire
2 silver mushroom beads, 6 mm
Stick pin

◆ **TOOLS & EQUIPMENT**

See "Copper Cat" above.

◆ **INSTRUCTIONS**

Making the Template:
Follow instructions for "Copper Cat" above.

Forming the Wire:
1. Cut a 12" piece of 16 gauge copper wire. Add silver beads to wire.
2. Bend wire in shape of template, beginning and ending in the muzzle area. (Fig. 2)
3. Cut two 12" pieces of 24 gauge silver wire for whiskers. See Steps 5-8 of "Copper Cat" for making whiskers and completing the stick pin. ∾

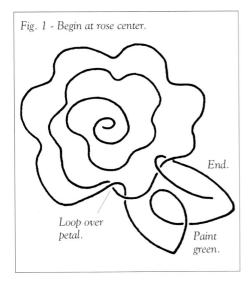

Fig. 1 - Begin at rose center.

Loop over petal.

End.

Paint green.

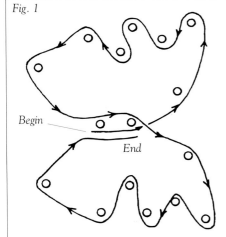

Fig. 1

Begin

End

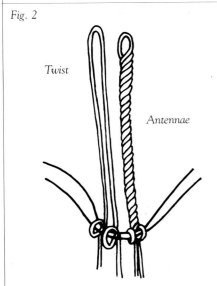

Fig. 2

Twist

Antennae

Sweet Rose

PIN

Pictured on page 35

Designed by Patty Cox

◆ SUPPLIES

17 gauge aluminum wire
Acrylic craft paint:
    Pink   Red
    Light green   Medium green
Clear acrylic spray finish
Pin back

◆ TOOLS & EQUIPMENT

Round clothespin   Round nose pliers
Needle nose pliers   Hammer
Anvil or brick   Jewelry glue
Flat artist's paint brush

◆ INSTRUCTIONS

Forming the Wire:
1. Cut an 18" piece of aluminum wire. Bend 1/4" at end of wire at a 90 degree angle. Place bent end of wire in slit in clothespin. Coil wire around clothespin. Remove wire from clothespin. (It will look like a spring.)
2. Clip off beginning bent end. Using round nose pliers, tighten center of coil. With your fingers, loosen wire curved around center, making a large, flat coil.
3. Using needle nose pliers, make a bend in the wire, form a curved petal, and make another bend. Continue around coil, bending and curving every 1/2". (Fig. 1)
4. Pull the last 3" of wire straight. Form leaves according to pattern, looping end of wire over petal. (Fig. 1)
5. Place wire shape on anvil, a brick, or a concrete surface. Hammer flat.

Painting & Finishing:
6. Dab pink and red paint on rose petals. See photo for color placement. Let dry.
7. Dab light green and medium green paint on stem and leaves. Let dry.
8. Spray with clear acrylic sealer. Let dry.
9. Attach pin back with glue. ∽

Silver Butterfly

STICK PIN

Pictured on page 35

Designed by Patty Cox

◆ SUPPLIES

16 gauge silver buss wire 24 gauge copper wire
24 gauge silver wire   Stick pin
Marquis rhinestone, 8mm x 18mm

◆ TOOLS & EQUIPMENT

18 small headless nails Wooden board
Hammer   Needle nose pliers
Tracing paper   Transfer paper and stylus
Jewelry glue

◆ INSTRUCTIONS

Making the Template:
1. Trace pattern for template. Transfer to board.
2. Hammer nails at markings. (Fig. 1)

Forming the Wire:
3. Cut a 24" piece of 16 gauge wire. Beginning at center, wrap wire around nails of template to make wings. (Fig. 1) End wire at center. Lift from template.
4. Cut two 5" pieces copper wire for antennae. Bend each piece in half. Loop around center of butterfly wings where wire crosses. Twist wires tightly. (Fig. 2)
5. Cut a 24" piece of 24 gauge silver wire. Starting bottom center, wrap tightly to form butterfly's body, covering ends of antennae.

Finishing:
6. Glue rhinestone at center.
7. Curve mounting post of stick pin with pliers. Glue on back of butterfly body. ∽

Dangling Star

PENDANT

Designed by Patty Cox

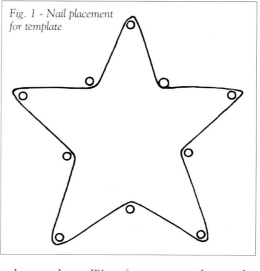
Fig. 1 - Nail placement for template

◆ SUPPLIES

16 gauge silver buss wire
24 gauge gold wire
Thin cording

◆ TOOLS & EQUIPMENT

11 small headless nails (3/4" wire brads
    work well)
Wooden board
Hammer
Needle nose pliers
Tracing paper
Transfer paper and stylus

◆ INSTRUCTIONS

Making the Template:
1. Trace pattern for template. Transfer to board.
2. Hammer nails at markings. (Fig. 1)

Forming the Wire:
3. Cut a 50" piece of 16 gauge wire. Starting at lower inside point of star, shape wire around nails, creating the star shape. Wrap four times, ending at the starting point. Remove wire shape from template.
4. Cut five pieces of 24 gauge gold wire, each 10" long. Wrap inner points of star with gold wire, tucking ends under wraps.

Finishing:
5. Loop cording through top of star. ∞

Silver Heart

STICK PIN

Designed by Patty Cox

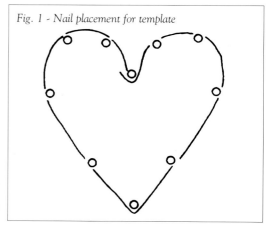
Fig. 1 - Nail placement for template

◆ SUPPLIES

16 gauge silver buss wire
20 gauge gold wire
24 gauge silver wire
Large safety pin
Earring back

◆ TOOLS & EQUIPMENT

10 small headless nails (3/4" wire brads
    work well)
Wooden board   Hammer
Needle nose pliers   Tracing paper
Transfer paper and stylus

◆ INSTRUCTIONS

Making the Template:
1. Trace pattern for template. Transfer to board.
2. Hammer nails at markings. (Fig. 1)

Forming the Wire:
3. Cut a 38" piece of 16 gauge wire. Make a bend in wire with pliers. Starting at upper inside point of heart, shape wire around nails, forming the outer curves of the heart shape. Wrap five times, ending at the starting point. Don't cut the end of the wire. Remove wire shape from template.
4. Wrap wire around upper inside point of heart, securing end and ending the wrap on the back.
5. Cut a 14" piece of 20 gauge gold wire. Wrap lower point of heart with gold wire, ending on the back.

Finishing:
6. Cut safety pin 3/8" above bottom coil. Save the sharp point of the pin.
7. Slide the 3/8" wire end of the pin through the wrapping on the upper back. Using needle nose pliers, bend the 3/8" end around the wrapped wire and the coiled part of the safety pin end.
8. Cut a 3" piece 24 gauge silver wire. Secure coiled end of safety pin to wrapped wire on back of heart. Clip ends.
9. Slide earring back on point of pin. ∞

Pictured from top: Oak Leaf Pin (instructions on page 42), Silver Heart Stick Pin (instructions on page 38), Dangling Star Pendant (instructions on page 38).

Watering Can

PIN

Designed by Patty Cox

♦ SUPPLIES

16 gauge silver buss wire
24 gauge silver wire
Stick pin

♦ TOOLS & EQUIPMENT

17 small headless nails (3/4" wire brads
    work well)
Wooden board
Hammer
Needle nose pliers
Tracing paper
Transfer paper and stylus
Tape

♦ INSTRUCTIONS

Making the Template:
1. Trace pattern for template. Transfer to
   board.
2. Hammer nails at markings. (Fig. 1)

Forming the Wire:
3. Cut a 36" piece of 16 gauge wire. Hold
   one end of wire with needle nose pliers.
   Coil 4" of wire into a spiral. Place spiral
   inside the nails that form the handle on
   the template.
4. Shape remaining wire around nails.
   Bend wire around nails to form outside
   curves; bend wire inside nails to form
   inside curves. Remove wire shape from
   template.
5. Cut three 6" lengths 24 gauge silver
   wire. Wrap 16 gauge wire together, using
   photo as a guide for placing the wraps.
   Secure ends and clip.

Finishing:
6. Cut the top of the stick pin, leaving a
   pointed 2-1/2" stick. Tape the top 1/4" of
   the stick pin to the handle area of the
   watering can.
7. Cut 6" 24 gauge wire. Wrap taped area of
   stick pin to watering can shape. ∽

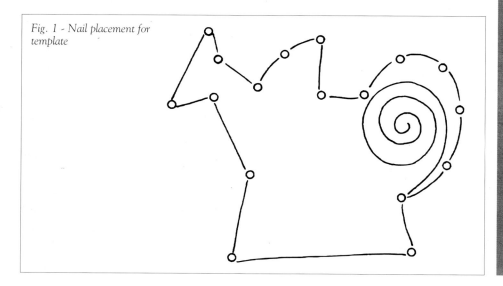

Fig. 1 - Nail placement for template

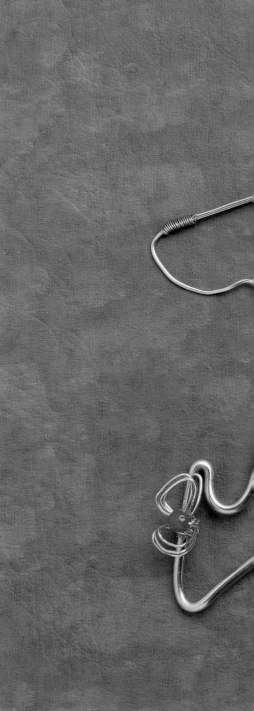

40

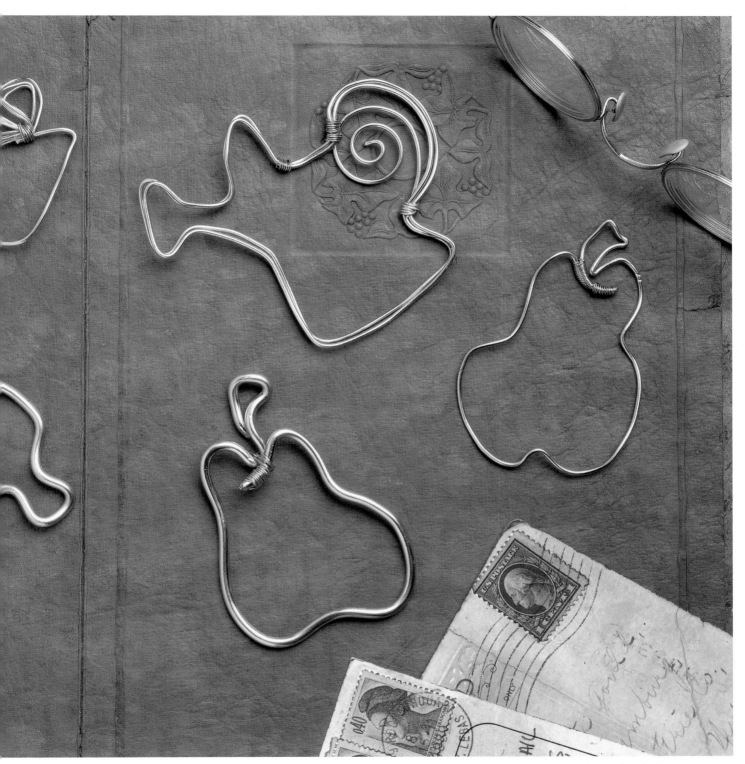

Pictured clockwise from top right: Watering Can Pin (instructions on page 40), Plump Pears Pin (instructions on page 42), Shoes with Style (instructions on page 43).

Oak Leaf

Pendant

Pictured on page 39

Designed by Patty Cox

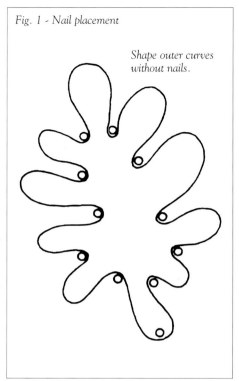

Fig. 1 - Nail placement

Shape outer curves without nails.

◆ **SUPPLIES**

16 gauge copper wire
24 gauge copper wire
Thin cording

◆ **TOOLS & EQUIPMENT**

11 small headless nails (3/4" wire brads
   work well)
Wooden board
Hammer
Needle nose pliers
Tracing paper
Transfer paper and stylus

◆ **INSTRUCTIONS**

Making the Template:
1. Trace pattern for template. Transfer to board.
2. Hammer nails at markings. (Fig. 1)

Forming the Wire:
3. Cut a 16" piece of 16 gauge wire. Starting at leaf stem, shape wire around template. Bend wire inside nails to form inside curves. shape outer curves of leaf as shown in Fig. 1. Remove wire from template.
4. Cut a 12" length of 24 gauge wire. Wrap around area where 16 gauge wire begins and ends. Secure and clip ends.

Finishing:
5. Loop cording through stem. ∽

Plump Pears

Pins

Pictured on pages 40-41

Designed by Patty Cox

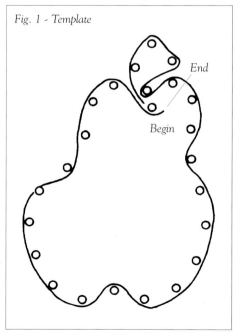

Fig. 1 - Template

End

Begin

◆ **SUPPLIES**

For thicker pin:
Lead-free plumbing solder wire, .081 gauge
20 gauge gold wire   Stick pin

For thinner pin:
16 gauge silver wire   24 gauge gold wire
Stick pin

◆ **TOOLS & EQUIPMENT**

23 small headless nails (3/4" wire brads
   work well)
Wooden board
Hammer
Flat nose pliers
Tracing paper
Transfer paper and stylus
Jewelry glue

◆ **INSTRUCTIONS**

Making the Template:
1. Trace pattern for template. Transfer to board.
2. Hammer nails at markings. (Fig. 1)

Forming the Wire:
For the thicker pin:
3. Cut a 10" piece of solder wire. Beginning at top center, wrap wire around nails of template. End wire at stem. Lift wire from template.
4. Cut a 7" piece 20 gauge gold wire. Wrap ends of solder wire to join. See photo.

For the thinner pin:
5. Cut a 10" piece of 16 gauge silver wire. Beginning at top center, wrap wire around nails of template. End wire at stem. Lift wire from template.
6. Cut a 7" piece 24 gauge gold wire. Wrap ends of silver wire to join. See photo.

Finishing:
7. Glue stick pins on backs of pears. ∽

Shoes with Style

Pins

Pictured on pages 40-41

Designed by Patty Cox

◆ SUPPLIES

For thicker pin:
Lead-free plumbing solder, .081 gauge
20 gauge gold wire
1 red bead, 12 mm
Stick pin

For thinner pin:
16 gauge silver buss wire
20 gauge gold wire
24 gauge silver wire
Large safety pin

◆ TOOLS & EQUIPMENT

19 small headless nails (3/4" wire brads
    work well)
Wooden board
Hammer
Flat nose pliers
Tracing paper
Transfer paper and stylus
Jewelry glue

◆ INSTRUCTIONS

Making the Template:
1. Trace pattern for template. Transfer to board.
2. Hammer nails at markings. (Fig. 1)

Forming the Wire:
For the thicker pin:
3. Cut a 12" piece of solder wire. Beginning at where the bow will be placed, wrap wire around nails of template. End wire at starting point.
4. Cut a 13" piece 20 gauge gold wire. Make three rounds of wire around bow shape. Lift wire from template.
5. Cut a 6" piece of 20 gauge gold wire. Thread red bead on center of wire. Place bead at center of bow. Wrap ends of gold wire around bow and shoe to join bow to shoe and to join ends of solder wire. Secure and clip ends. Add a drop of glue to secure.

For the thinner pin:
6. Cut a 12" piece of 16 gauge wire. Beginning at where the bow will be placed, wrap wire around nails of template. End wire at starting point.
7. Cut a 13" piece 20 gauge gold wire. Make three rounds of wire around bow shape. Lift wire from template.
8. Cut a 6" piece 24 gauge silver wire. Wrap bow to shoe, joining beginning and end of shoe wire. Secure ends and clip. Add a drop of glue to secure.

Finishing:
For thicker pin:
9. Glue stick pin on back of shoe. ∽

For thinner pin:
10. Cut off pointed part of safety pin to use as stick pin.
11. Align stick pin with shoe top. Cut a 6" piece of 24 gauge silver wire. Secure stick pin to shoe by wrapping end with wire.
12. Add a drop of glue to secure. ∽

Fig. 1 - Nail placement for template

Wire Works Bottles & Vases

Simple glass bottles and vases—clear or colored—can be transformed using wire and stones into special works of art. Use them as decorative items all by themselves, or use them to hold flowers, vinegars, cooking oil, liqueurs, wine at the dinner table, or bubble bath on your dressing table. ∾

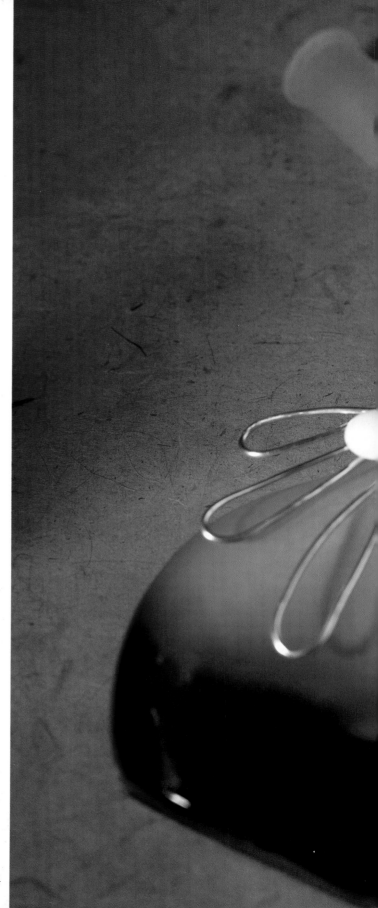

Magenta & Swirls

DECORATIVE BOTTLE

Designed by Vivian Peritts

◆ SUPPLIES

Frosted magenta glass bottle, 12-1/2" tall
Cork to fit bottle
1 clear glass cabochon, 1" dia.
1 frosted crystal round bead, 10 mm
1 unichite disc, 14 mm
1 frosted grape oval bead, 14 x 10 mm
14 gauge aluminum armature wire, 9'
20 gauge aluminum wire, 12"

◆ TOOLS & EQUIPMENT

Wire cutters
Needle nose pliers
Jewelry or metal glue

◆ INSTRUCTIONS

Decorating the Cork:
1. Cut an 8" piece of 14 gauge wire. Make a coil that is 1" diameter. (Fig. 1) Leave a 2" tail as shown in figure.
2. Thread the frosted crystal round bead, the unichite disc, and the frosted grape oval bead onto the 2" end of wire.
3. Tightly coil a piece of wire to make a coil the diameter of the top of the cork. See the General Instructions for information on making flat coils. Glue coil flat on top of the cork.
4. In the top of the cork at center of glued coil, make a hole for the beaded wire coil. Drip some glue in hole. Insert beaded coil in the hole. Let dry.

Decorating the Bottle:
5. Cut a piece of 14 gauge wire 24" long. Form coils at both ends, using Fig. 2 as a pattern. Wrap the wire around the neck of the bottle, positioning it about halfway up the neck. The coiled ends should be at the front of the bottle.
6. Cut a 20" piece of 14 gauge wire. Coil and bend, using Fig. 3 as a pattern. Set aside.
7. Cut another 20" piece of 14 gauge wire. Make a 1" loop in the center. Twist to secure. Coil both ends of the wire. Place the wire, loop down, at the bottom of the neck of the bottle and wrap the wire around the bottom of the neck. The coiled ends should be at the front of the bottle.
8. Slip the coiled and bent wire (Fig. 3) through the loop.
9. Wrap the clear glass cabochon with 12" of 20 gauge wire, leaving a 1" tail on each end. Apply some glue to back of cabochon to secure to wire. Let dry.
10. Use tails of wire that is wrapping the cabochon to attach cabochon to wire loop. ᖇ

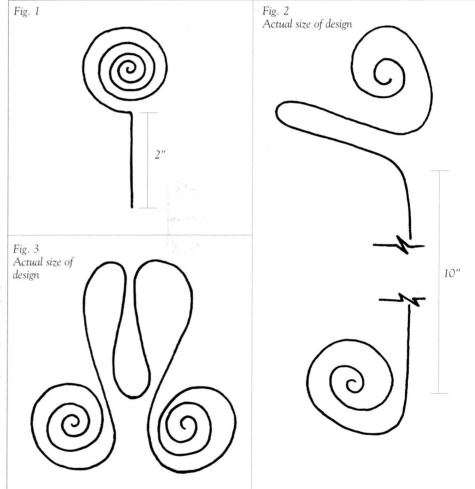

Fig. 1

Fig. 2
Actual size of design

2"

Fig. 3
Actual size of design

10"

Sapphire Frost

Decorative Bottle

Designed by Vivian Peritts

◆ SUPPLIES

Frosted blue glass bottle, 12-1/2" tall
Cork to fit bottle
Round wooden ball with one flattened side,
    1-1/4" diameter (sold as a doll's head)
Acrylic craft paint, blue (to match color
    of bottle)
Milk glass cabochon, 3/4" dia.
14 gauge aluminum armature wire, 9'
20 gauge aluminum wire, 6"

◆ TOOLS & EQUIPMENT

Wire cutters
Needle nose pliers
Jewelry or metal glue

◆ INSTRUCTIONS

Decorating the Cork:
1. Paint wooden ball with blue paint. Let dry.
2. Glue flattened side of wooden ball to top of cork.
3. Cut a 12" piece of 14 gauge wire. Tightly coil one end. Place the coil on top of the wooden ball and wind the wire loosely around the ball and cork to about the halfway point of the cork piece. (Fig. 1)

Decorating the Bottle:
4. Cut a 3' piece of 14 gauge wire. Bend and coil wire, using Fig. 2 as a pattern.
5. Cut a 6" piece of 20 gauge wire. Wrap around wire shape as shown in Fig. 2.
6. Cut a 24" piece of 14 gauge wire. Coil both ends.
7. Position the wire shape (Fig. 2) on the front of the bottle at the bottom of the neck. Wrap the 24" piece with coiled ends from step 3 around the bottom of the neck of the bottle and the wire shape, securing the wire shape on the bottle. Finish with one coiled end pointing up and the other pointing down. See photo.
8. Glue the milk glass cabochon on the wire shape, using photo as a guide for placement. ◌

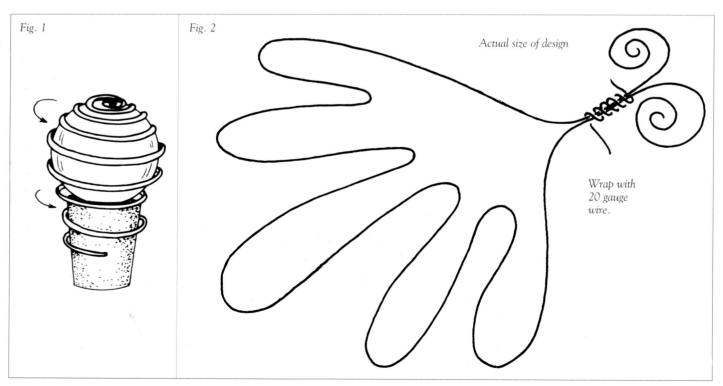

Fig. 1

Fig. 2

Actual size of design

Wrap with 20 gauge wire.

Circles & Gems

BUD VASE

Designed by Patty Cox

◆ SUPPLIES

Clear glass bud vase, 7-1/2" tall
16 gauge silver buss wire, 60"
9 frosted cabochons, 1/2", in various
    colors
6 clear glass cabochons, 3/4"

Fig. 1

◆ TOOLS & EQUIPMENT

Flat coil maker (see General Instructions)
Epoxy glue
Toothpicks

◆ INSTRUCTIONS

1. Cut three 20" lengths of silver wire. Make three flat coils, each 1" in diameter, using Flat Coil Maker, at the end of each length. There will be a long tail on end of coil.
2. Position coils, one at a time, on bud vase. Slightly curve coils to conform to shape of vase. Shape wire tails to wrap around vase. (Fig. 1)
3. Arrange and glue coils on vase, curving wire tails around vase and using photo as a guide. (Glue does not need to be applied to wire tails.)
4. Glue one frosted cabochon at the center of each coil.
5. Glue remaining frosted cabochons and clear cabochons randomly on vase, using photo as a guide.

TIPS:

• Mix a small amount of epoxy glue at a time.
• Use a toothpick to apply glue to coils and stones.
• Work one side of the vase at a time.
• Glue cabochons at ends of wire tails to secure and obscure them. ⌒

Wire Works Tabletop Glamour

Use wire to turn everyday items into terrific tabletop accessories. In this chapter, you'll see how plastic-handled flatware, simple salt and pepper shakers, a shiny chrome shaker, and clear glass goblets are transformed with wire, beads, and stones. You'll also find instructions for making napkin rings and place card holders. Gentle hand washing is recommended for all tabletop projects. ∾

Spirals & Curves

FLATWARE & NAPKIN RING

Casual plastic-handled flatware gets dressed up with silver wire and frosted cabochons. A coordinating wire napkin ring completes the look.

Designed by Patty Cox

◆ SUPPLIES

1 place setting stainless steel flatware with colored plastic handles
16 gauge silver buss wire
3 frosted cabochons, 1/2" dia, in three different colors

◆ TOOLS & EQUIPMENT

Round nose pliers
Jewelry or metal glue
Round cylinder shape for shaping napkin ring, 1" to 1-1/4" in diameter (a dowel, for example)

◆ INSTRUCTIONS

Decorating the Flatware:
1. Cut a 13" piece of wire for each piece of flatware.
2. Grasp one end of a wire piece with round nose pliers. Make a small coil (two rounds).
3. Place the small coil on a piece of flatware at the top of the handle. Spiral wire around handle five times.
4. Grasp end of wire with pliers and coil tightly at bottom of handle. See photo.
5. Glue a frosted cabochon onto handle as shown in photo.
6. Repeat steps 2-6 for each piece of flatware.

Making the Napkin Ring:
1. Cut a 20" piece of wire.
2. Grasp one end of the wire with round nose pliers. Make a small coil (two rounds).
3. Hold the small coil on top of the cylinder shape and wrap wire diagonally around cylinder four times, leaving a 4" tail.
4. Grasp end of wire with pliers and coil. See photo. ∞

Pair of Partners

SALT & PEPPER SHAKERS

*A pair of salt and pepper shakers is dressed up with wire and glass cabochons.
Choose a color for the cabochons that coordinates with your decor.*

Designed by Patty Cox

◆ SUPPLIES

Flat-sided clear glass salt & pepper shakers
    with silver tops
Lead-free silver solder wire
8 cobalt blue glass cabochons, 3/4" dia

◆ TOOLS & EQUIPMENT

Round nose pliers
Epoxy glue

◆ INSTRUCTIONS

1. Cut an 8" piece of solder wire. Grasp end with round nose pliers. Form a tight coil.
   (Fig. 1) Shape wire according to Fig. 1, wrapping it around a glass cabochon and coiling the tail.
2. Repeat step 1 seven times, for a total of eight designs.
3. Glue one cabochon with wire design on each side of the shakers. ∾

Fig. 1

glass cabochon here

Sugar & Spice

SHAKER

Use this shaker for cinnamon, powdered sugar, or cocoa in your kitchen. It is a great accessory to your cappuccino paraphernalia. Or fill it with bath powder for an elegant bathroom accessory.

Designed by Patty Cox

◆ **SUPPLIES**

Silver shaker, 4-1/2" tall, 2-3/4" diameter
16 gauge copper wire
9 round crystal acrylic beads, 8 mm
7 round crystal acrylic beads, 5 mm

◆ **TOOLS & EQUIPMENT**

Flat coil maker (See General Instructions)
Epoxy glue
Large rubber bands

◆ **INSTRUCTIONS**

1. Cut six pieces copper wire, 18-24" long. (Varying the lengths will make coils of slightly different sizes.) Make six s-shaped double flat coils, using Flat Coil Maker. See Fig. 1.
2. Cut six pieces copper wire, 6-10" long, again varying the lengths to make coils of different sizes. Make six flat coils, using Flat Coil Maker.
3. Press coils on shaker to slightly conform coils to the shape of the shaker.
4. Position and glue coils on shaker. Hold coils in place with rubber bands until glue dries. When dry, remove rubber bands.
5. Glue a crystal bead in the center of each coil. ෨

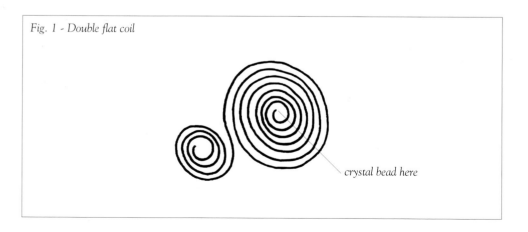

Fig. 1 - Double flat coil

crystal bead here

Beads & Glamour

DECORATED GOBLETS

These goblets will add sparkle and color to your table. Ours are made with both gold and silver wire and lots of beads in assorted colors. For a different look, use all gold or all silver wire. Or choose beads in all one color or in just a few colors to accent your dishes.

◆ SUPPLIES

2 clear glass stemmed goblets
100 glass beads, 3 mm, various colors
20 gauge silver wire
24 gauge gold wire
Epoxy glue

◆ TOOLS & EQUIPMENT

Wire cutters

◆ INSTRUCTIONS

1. Starting at the base of the goblet stem, spiral silver wire tightly up the stem. When you get to the top, coil the wire back down to the bottom of the stem to make a criss-cross design. Cut wire. Secure ends of wire at base, by twisting together and tucking cut ends under.
2. Cut a 24" piece of gold wire. Twist end of gold wire around silver wire at base to secure. Thread a bead on the wire. Wrap wire on stem around silver wire, adding a bead every half turn or so. (The gold wire crossing the silver wire holds the beads in place.) Continue wrapping the wire and adding beads.
3. When you get to the top of the stem, spiral gold wire back down the stem to the bottom, adding more beads as you go down stem. Cut wire when you reach the bottom. Twists ends and tuck under to secure. (You want to be able to pick up the glass without getting stuck with a cut end of wire.)
4. A few spots of epoxy at top of spiral will secure the wrap. ∽

Flower Garden

PLACE CARD FAVORS

Use these holders on the table for place cards or photos, and let your guests take them home when the party's over. Vary the colors to suit your table.

Designed by Sonny Knox

Daisy In A Pot

◆ SUPPLIES

16 gauge steel baling wire
Clay flower pot, 3/4" diameter
Plaster of Paris
Fine sand
Green moss or excelsior
Gloss sealer spray
Spray paint:
　Yellow
　Green
　White primer
Acrylic craft paint:
　Orange
　Light green

◆ TOOLS & EQUIPMENT

Glue gun and glue sticks
Needle nose pliers
Small natural sponge
Broom handle (medium size)
Damp cloth or paper towel
Piece of cardboard (to use as a paint
　shield)
Flat artist's paint brush
Disposable foam plate or palette

◆ INSTRUCTIONS

Forming the Daisy:
1. Cut a piece of wire 60" long. Straighten out all the kinks. Wipe wire with a damp cloth or paper towel.
2. With pliers, form a spiral 3/4" in diameter at one end of wire, leaving a long tail of wire at the other end.
3. Hold the spiral against a broom handle and coil the remaining wire around the handle, creating a loose spring. Make nine or ten loops, keeping 3/4" between turns. You will still have a long tail of wire remaining.
4. Remove wire from handle. Take the spring and flatten it in the same plane as the spiral. Form the flattened spring around the spiral, which is the flower center, creating the petals. (See Fig. 1 on page 65.)
5. Lay the flower on the pattern and shape if necessary. With tail of wire, form the stem and the leaves. To keep the design flat, do not cross wires. Use pliers to pinch and form the tips of the leaves.
6. Form the end of the wire in a loose spring to anchor it in the pot.

Painting & Finishing:
7. Spray the inside of the flower pot with gloss sealer. Let dry.
8. Spray the formed wire with white primer. Let dry.
9. Spray the stem and leaves of the wire flower with green paint. Let dry.
10. Use a piece of cardboard to shield the leaves and stem. Spray the flower with yellow paint. Let dry.
11. Paint the flower center and the flower pot orange. Let dry.
12. Dampen the sponge. Squeeze out excess water. Pour a little light green paint on a palette or disposable plate. Dip sponge in paint. Press sponge over flower pot to create a mottled look. Also sponge the leaf tips with light green. Let dry.
13. Mix plaster of Paris according to package instructions, adding a bit of fine sand to make the mixture heavier. Place the spring anchor end of the wire flower in pot. Add enough plaster mix to fill the pot 3/4" from the top. Let dry.
14. Spray the flower and pot with gloss sealer. Let dry.
15. Glue shreds of green moss or excelsior on the surface of the plaster. ❦

See pattern for "Daisy in a Pot" on page 65 and instructions for "Rose in a Pot" on page 64.

Flower Garden

PLACE CARD FAVORS

Designed by Sonny Knox

Rose In A Pot
Pictured on page 63

◆ SUPPLIES

16 gauge steel baling wire
Clay flower pot, 3/4" diameter
Plaster of Paris
Fine sand
Green moss or excelsior
Gloss sealer spray
Spray paint:
    Dark red
    Green
    White primer
Acrylic craft paint:
    Pink
    Yellow
    Light green

◆ TOOLS & EQUIPMENT

Glue gun and glue sticks
Needle nose pliers
Small natural sponge
Broom handle (medium size)
Damp cloth or paper towel
Piece of cardboard (to use as a paint
    shield)
Flat artist's paint brush
Disposable foam plate or palette

◆ INSTRUCTIONS

Forming the Rose:
1. Cut a piece of wire 50" long. Straighten out all the kinks. Wipe wire with a damp cloth or paper towel.
2. With pliers, form a spiral 1-1/4" in diameter for the flower center at one end of the wire length.
3. Following the pattern, form the outer petals, crimping the points with pliers. (See Fig. 2.)
4. Lay the flower on the pattern and form the stem and the leaves. To keep the design flat, do not cross wires. Use pliers to pinch and shape the tips of the leaves.
5. Form the end of the wire in a loose spring to anchor it in the pot.

Painting & Finishing:
6. Spray the inside of the flower pot with gloss sealer. Let dry.
7. Spray the formed wire with white primer. Let dry.
8. Spray the stem and leaves of the wire flower with green paint. Let dry.
9. Use a piece of cardboard to shield the leaves and stem. Spray the flower with dark red paint. Let dry.
10. Paint the flower center pink. Let dry.
11. Paint the flower pot yellow. Let dry.
12. Dampen the sponge. Squeeze out excess water. Pour a little light green paint on a palette or disposable plate. Dip sponge in paint. Press sponge over flower pot to create a mottled look. Also sponge the leaf tips with light green. Let dry.
13. Mix plaster of Paris according to package instructions, adding a bit of fine sand to make the mixture heavier. Place the spring anchor end of the wire flower in pot. Add enough plaster mix to fill the pot 3/4" from the top. Let dry.
14. Spray the flower and pot with gloss sealer. Let dry.
15. Glue shreds of green moss or excelsior on the surface of the plaster. ∽

Fig. 1 - Pattern for Daisy

Fig. 2 - Pattern for Rose

Deco Diamonds

PLACE CARD HOLDERS

♦ SUPPLIES

Silver armature wire, 1/8" diameter
Glass cabochons, 3/4", assorted colors

♦ TOOLS & EQUIPMENT

Round nose pliers
Wire cutters
Epoxy glue

♦ INSTRUCTIONS

1. Cut a piece of wire, 30" long for each holder you are making.
2. Place one piece of wire on pattern A (Fig. 1) and form wire, working from one end, to fit pattern.
3. Continue bending wire into a triangular spiral, following pattern B.
4. Bend the top so the upper triangle is suspended above the larger triangle (Fig. 2).
5. Glue a glass cabochon at the center of the upper triangles.
6. Repeat steps 2-5, using remaining pieces of wire and remaining cabochons for as many holders as you wish to make. ෨

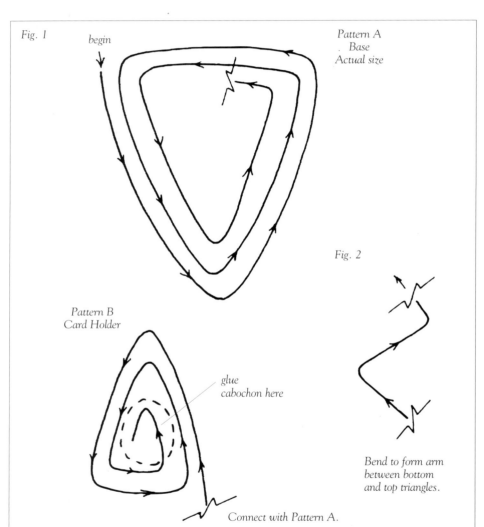

Fig. 1

begin

Pattern A
Base
Actual size

Fig. 2

Pattern B
Card Holder

glue
cabochon here

Bend to form arm
between bottom
and top triangles.

Connect with Pattern A.

Golden Mesh Bow

NAPKIN RING

Designed by Patty Cox

◆ SUPPLIES

40 gauge bronze wire mesh screen, 36" wide

◆ TOOLS & EQUIPMENT

Old scissors or metal shears
Jewelry or metal glue

◆ INSTRUCTIONS

1. Using old scissors or metal shears, cut a 2" x 36" piece of wire mesh.
2. Turn long edges under 1/4". Press folds with scissors handle.
3. Cut two pieces, one 5" long (for the ring) and one 3" long, off one end. (The remaining large piece should be 28" long.)
4. Turn remaining raw edges of all pieces under 1/4". Press flat with scissors handle.
5. Fold all pieces in half along their lengths. Press folds flat with scissors handle.
6. Find center of 28" strip. Form loops for bow, pinching mesh at center. (Fig. 1)
7. Shape tails of bow. (Fig. 2)
8. Shape 5" strip and 3" strips into rings. Place the larger ring under the bow shape with the ends of the ring under the center of the bow. Loop the shorter ring around the center of the bow, covering the ends of the larger ring underneath. Glue the ends of the bow loop together to secure ends and hold larger ring to bow. ∾

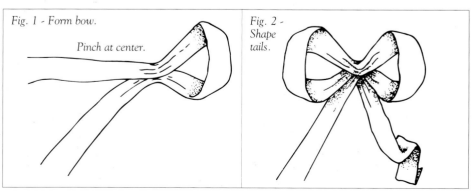

Fig. 1 - Form bow.

Pinch at center.

Fig. 2 - Shape tails.

Circles & Stones

NAPKIN RINGS

Designed by Marion Brizendine

◆ SUPPLIES

16 gauge steel wire
18 gauge brass wire
Optional: Glass bead or
   cabochon, 3/4"

◆ TOOLS & EQUIPMENT

Needle nose pliers
Round object for shaping wire
   ring (bottom of a small glass,
   a large dowel, the neck of a
   milk jug)

◆ INSTRUCTIONS

1. Cut an 18" piece of steel wire.
   Shape wire three times around
   a round object to make a ring
   about 2" in diameter.
2. Cut a 5" piece of 18 gauge
   brass wire. Wrap around ring
   where ends cross to secure
   ring. Curl or twist ends as you
   like.
3. Curl or twist ends of steel wire,
   using photo as a guide.
4. *Optional:* Wrap a glass bead or
   cabochon with steel wire.
   Twist tail ends of wire tightly
   and loop around ring to
   secure. ∾

Wire Works Lamps & Shades

Brighten a corner or give your dinner table the romantic feel of an intimate cafe with a wire-decorated lampshade or lamp. In this chapter, you'll find innovative styles to complement traditional and contemporary interiors, including a decorated paper shade with a Southwestern look, a woven wire shade with beads and prisms that has a Victorian feel, and a simple pleated shade made with wire mesh. ∾

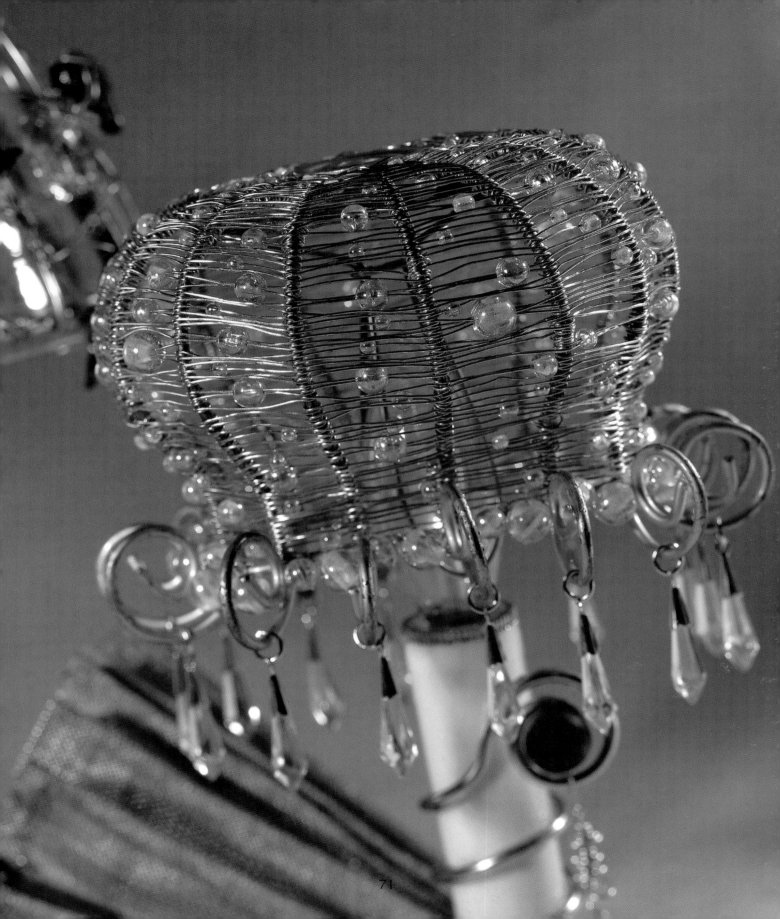

Shades of Art

LAMPSHADE

Stained glass pieces wrapped with wire adorn the clear glass shade of a candle lamp.

Designed by Vivian Peritts

◆ SUPPLIES

Clear glass cafe lamp with clear glass shade
16 gauge brass wire, 12'
24 gauge copper wire, 50'
2" silver metal ring
5" silver metal ring
24 colored stained glass pieces, assorted colors and shapes (pieces range in size from approximately 1" x 1" to 1-1/2" x 1")

◆ TOOLS & EQUIPMENT

Wire cutters
Round nose pliers
Jewelry glue

◆ INSTRUCTIONS

1. Cut 12 pieces of wire, each 12" long.
2. Wrap one end of each wire three or four times around the 2" ring.
3. Place the 2" ring with the 12 wires attached on top of the glass shade. Select four wires—one in each quadrant of the shade—and use them to connect the 2" ring and the 5" ring. The 5" ring should be at the level of the bottom of the glass shade. Wrap the wires around the rings as many times as needed so the ring hangs straight.
4. Wrap the remaining eight brass wires onto the bottom ring. The middle sections of these wires can be loose, with kinks and bends in them, to give the shade form.
5. Cut a 24" long piece of copper wire for each piece of stained glass. Wrap the center of one wire three or four times around one piece of glass. You will have tails of wire left at each end of the glass piece. Put a dot of glue on the back of the glass piece where the wire touches it to hold the wire in place. Repeat with remaining pieces of glass and wire. Let glue dry.
6. Wrap the ends of the copper wires (holding glass pieces) randomly around the brass wires and the wire rings, overlapping and looping the copper wires to create a webbed look over the glass lampshade and spacing the glass pieces over the shade. ∾

Touch of the West

LAMPSHADE

Wire and beads give a Southwestern feel to a simple paper lampshade.

Designed by Beth Cosner

◆ SUPPLIES

Natural paper lampshade, 7" tall, 4" diameter at top, 7" diameter at bottom
14 round red wooden beads, 12 mm
14 golden brown pony beads, 6 x 9 mm
Lead-free silver solid solder, .081 gauge

◆ TOOLS & EQUIPMENT

Drill and 5/64" drill bit
Face shield or safety goggles
Glue gun and glue sticks
Wire cutters
Flat nose pliers
Measuring tape or ruler
Pencil
Old hand towel

Fig. 1

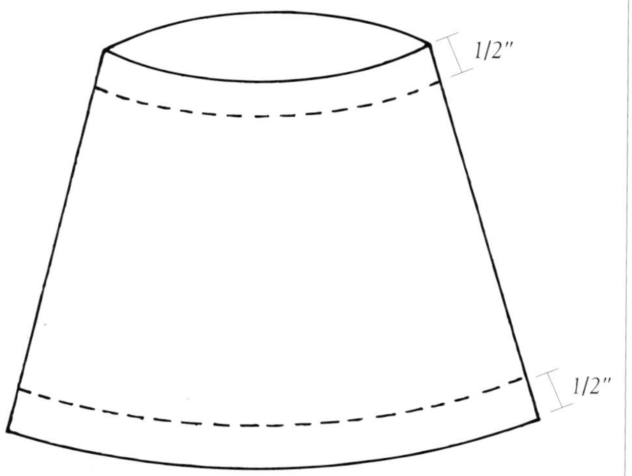

Fig. 2

1/2"

1/2"

◆ INSTRUCTIONS

Measuring & Marking:
1. Measure down 1/2" from the top of the shade, around the entire circumference. Draw a light pencil line at this point around shade.
2. Measure up 1/2" from the bottom of the shade around the entire circumference. Draw a light pencil line.
3. On the line drawn at top of shade, measure and make marks at 1" intervals around shade.
4. Drill a 5/64" hole at each mark.
5. Cut seven pieces of solder wire, each 14", for use with the red beads. Cut seven pieces of solder wire, each 12-1/2", for use with golden brown beads.
6. Place a piece of 14" wire in the upper hole. Hold the wire straight and mark the place where the wire crosses the marked line near the bottom of the shade. Repeat, marking the placement of the corresponding hole near the bottom of the shade for each hole around the top.
7. Drill 5/64" holes at the marks.

Adding the Wire & Beads:
Follow the same procedure for each wire piece and bead.
8. Make a loop at one end of a 14" piece of wire. Twist the end to secure. (Fig. 2)
9. Thread the unlooped end of the wire through the hole from the inside to the outside.
10. Bend the loop over the top of the shade. Thread the wire through the loop. Thread a red bead on the wire, positioning it on the shade over the hole. Glue the bead in place.
11. Straighten the wire by holding it with a towel and rubbing the towel up and down the wire.
12. Thread another red bead on the wire. Pass the end of wire through bottom hole from the outside to the inside. Position the bead over the hole and glue in place.
13. Loop the end of the wire around the bead and curve it around the bottom of the shade.
14. Repeat steps 8-13 with remaining wire pieces and beads. Alternate 14" wire pieces and red beads with 12-1/2" pieces of wire and golden brown beads around the shade. ∞

Wire & Mesh

LAMPSHADE & LAMP BASE

A battery-powered candle lamp is decorated with beds and wire. Pleated bronze mesh makes a simple, traditional shade.

Designed by Patty Cox

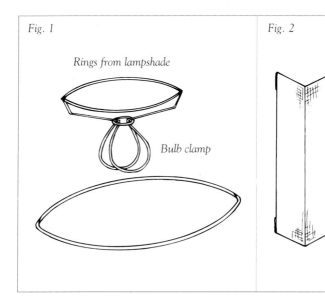

Fig. 1

Rings from lampshade

Bulb clamp

Fig. 2

Make holes in mesh with a T-pin.

◆ SUPPLIES

For the shade:
40 gauge bronze wire mesh, 36" x 4-1/2"
24 gauge gold wire
Paper lampshade with two rings, one 2-1/2" and one 5", with bulb clamp for candle lamp

For the lamp base:
Candlestick lamp base with clear bulb
Silver armature wire or silver lead-free solder wire, 1/8" dia.
2 frosted gold beads, 18 mm
Frosted teal cabochon, 1/2"
Gold wire eyepin

◆ TOOLS & EQUIPMENT

For the shade:
T-pin
Old scissors or metal shears
Metal & plastic cement
2 craft sticks
2 spring paper clamps or spring clothes pins

For the lamp base:
Epoxy glue
Round nose pliers
Toothpick

◆ INSTRUCTIONS

Making the Shade:
1. Fold long raw edges of wire mesh under 1/4". Run a craft stick over folds to press flat.
2. Accordion fold the mesh every 3/4", making the folds parallel to the short ends.
3. Apply glue to last fold on one short end. Overlap glue with other short end of mesh. Clamp glued ends together, placing craft sticks on the inside and outside of the glued area and using clamps or clothes pins to hold the craft sticks. Allow glue to dry.
4. Trim top and bottom metal rings from paper lampshade. (Fig. 1) Open accordion-folded mesh to fit rings.
5. Using a T-pin, make tiny holes on inner folds of mesh 1/4" from top and bottom edges. (Fig. 2)
6. Loop 24 gauge wire through holes and around lampshade rings to secure folded wire mesh to rings.

Decorating the Base:
1. Cut a 24" piece armature wire or solder wire. Grip one end of wire with round nose pliers. Make a 1" coil.
2. Wrap wire diagonally five times around shaft of candlestick lamp. Coil end of wire as shown in photo.
3. Slide coils 1/8" above desired placement on shaft. Apply glue with a toothpick just below the wires. Slide wires down on glue. Allow to dry.
4. Glue the teal cabochon in the center of the upper coil. Glue one gold bead in the center of the lower coil. Allow glue to dry.
5. Thread remaining bead onto the eyepin. Hang dangle from the upper coil. ∾

Woven Shade

LAMPSHADE

A wire downspout strainer is the base for this fanciful shade that's woven with wire and a multitude of crystal acrylic beads and trimmed with crystal prisms.

Designed by Patty Cox

◆ SUPPLIES

Downspout strainer to fit a 3" downspout (available at hardware stores and lumber yards)
1 spool 24 gauge gold wire
200 round crystal acrylic beads, assorted sizes (1/8" - 3/8")
15 acrylic prisms, 1" long, with gold caps
Paper lampshade with upper ring and bulb clamp for candle lamp
Candlestick lamp base with clear bulb

◆ TOOLS & EQUIPMENT

Needle nose pliers
Epoxy glue
Toothpick

◆ INSTRUCTIONS

1. With needle nose pliers, bend the end of each wire into a coil to form the upper edge of the lampshade.
2. Cut 1 yd. 24 gauge wire. Starting at what will be the top of the lampshade, wrap wire around one wire rib of the shade to secure. Thread wire over next rib, and wrap wire around rib once. Continue around basket, wrapping the wire around the ribs, covering the wire frame. Thread a bead onto wire between the wraps every so often.

TIPS:
- When you come to the end of a piece of wire, wrap the end tightly around a rib. Pinch with pliers and trim end. To start another, cut a piece of wire, wrap it around the rib, pinch with pliers to secure, and continue to wrap and add beads.
- When working with larger beads, thread wire through hole of bead from previous round to keep wrapping close together.
- When you get to the bottom of the shade, wrap end of wire securely and trim end.

3. Remove top ring and bulb clamp from paper lampshade. Place bulb clamp and ring on bulb. Apply epoxy glue to top of ring. Position shade over ring. Let glue dry. Option: Secure ring to shade with wire.
4. Attach a row of beads around bottom of shade with wire.
5. Slide a prism on each coil. ࠲

Wire Works Frames

Wire can be used to decorate purchased picture frames, to create an elegant swirled frame around a mirror or a clear acrylic frame, and to create a holder for photos that are close to your heart. Interesting options abound in this chapter. ∾

Suede & Spirals

PHOTO FRAME

Designed by Patty Cox

◆ SUPPLIES

White foam core board, 1/4" thick, 8"
  square
Black foam core board, 7" x 3"
Armature wire, 1/8" dia.
Metallic gold spray paint
Clear acrylic picture frame, 3-1/2" square
10" x 10" piece brown suede
7-1/2" square black paper

◆ TOOLS & EQUIPMENT

Needle nose pliers
Masking tape
Rubber cement
Household cement
Craft knife

◆ INSTRUCTIONS

Covering the Foam Core:
1. Apply rubber cement evenly to back side of suede. Center foam core piece on suede. Press, being sure suede is smooth.
2. Pull corners taut and tape to back of foam core with masking tape. Pull sides taut and tape, then pull top and bottom taut and tape.
3. Glue 7-1/2" piece of black paper to back to cover cut edges.
4. Cut an easel from black foam core. Score with a craft knife, cutting through paper on one side, so easel will bend. Glue to center back of suede-covered board with household cement.

Decorating:
5. Glue acrylic frame at center on front of suede-covered board, using household cement.
6. Cut eight 14" pieces armature wire. Hold the tip of one length with needle nose pliers and coil wire according to Fig. 1. Press coil flat.
7. Make a total of eight coils.
8. Spray coils with gold paint. Let dry.
9. Glue coils around acrylic frame with household cement. Place a heavy book on frame until glue dries. ∽

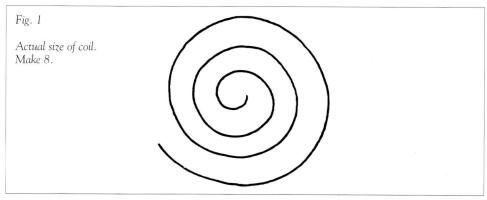

Fig. 1

Actual size of coil.
Make 8.

Stones & Swirls

PHOTO FRAME

Designed by Patty Cox

◆ SUPPLIES

Metal picture frame, 5-3/8" x 6-3/4" (2-1/2" x 4" opening)
Solid lead-free silver solder wire, .081 gauge
12 red glass cabochons, 3/4"
Chrome spray paint
Metallic gold rub-on wax

◆ TOOLS & EQUIPMENT

Round nose pliers
Epoxy glue

◆ INSTRUCTIONS

1. Cut a 7" piece of solder wire. Grasp one end with round nose pliers. Wrap enough of the wire tightly to make a 1" coil. Wrap remaining wire around a red glass cabochon, tucking end of wire under the coil. (Fig. 1) Make seven more coil-and-cabochon combinations for a total of eight.
2. Wrap remaining four cabochons with pieces of solder wire. Cut ends evenly and press wire ends together.
3. Remove cabochons from wire shapes. Spray frame and shaped wire pieces with chrome paint. Let dry.
4. Replace cabochons in wire shapes. Position on frame, using photo as a guide for placement.
5. Apply epoxy glue on backs of coils and cabochons. Glue on frame. Let dry.
6. Rub metallic gold wax on frame and coil edges. ∽

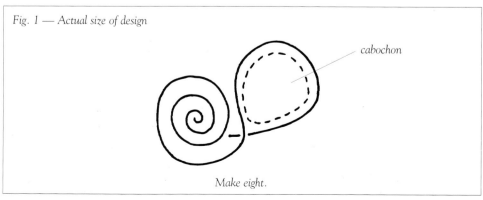

Fig. 1 — Actual size of design

cabochon

Make eight.

Victorian Swirls

PHOTO FRAME

Designed by Patty Cox

◆ SUPPLIES

Silver armature wire, 1/8" dia., 11'
24 gauge gold wire
Acrylic picture frame, 5" x 7"
Adhesive picture hanger

◆ TOOLS & EQUIPMENT

Needle nose pliers
Hammer
20 finishing nails
Wooden board, 1 x 6, 10" long
Craft knife & straight edge
Jewelry cement
T-pin & candle
Tracing paper
Transfer paper & stylus

◆ INSTRUCTIONS

Making the Template:
Armature wire bends easily, but to make eight identical shapes, it's helpful to make a template.
1. Trace pattern. (Fig. 1) Transfer to board.
2. Nail headless nails about every 3/8" along s-shape. (Fig. 2)

Preparing the Acrylic Frame:
Most acrylic frames have a bent acrylic stand on the back. If your frame has one, here's how to remove it:
3. Place frame on flat surface, face down.
4. Hold straight edge along bottom of frame just above where stand bends.
5. Using a very sharp craft knife, score acrylic with three strokes. Snap off bottom of frame with needle nose pliers.

Use a T-pin that's been heated in a candle flame to make pin holes on sides of frame:
6. Mark sides of frame 1" from each corner.
7. Light candle. Hold tip of T-pin over candle flame for 10 seconds. Press pin to mark on frame. The heat will melt the frame, making a tiny hole.

Continued on page 88

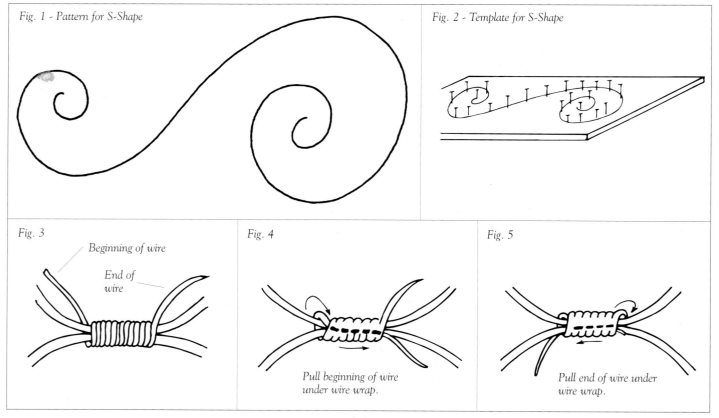

Fig. 1 - Pattern for S-Shape

Fig. 2 - Template for S-Shape

Fig. 3
Beginning of wire
End of wire

Fig. 4
Pull beginning of wire under wire wrap.

Fig. 5
Pull end of wire under wire wrap.

Victorian Swirls

PHOTO FRAME

Pictured on page 87

continued from page 86

8. Repeat for remaining three holes.

Making the Wire Shapes:
9. Cut eight 12" lengths of armature wire.
10. Make a tight coil at one end of one piece of wire with needle nose pliers. Place coiled end of wire over beginning nail on template. Shape wire around nails. Remove wire from template.
11. Repeat step 10 with remaining seven pieces of wire to make eight s-shapes in all.
12. Compare shapes, adjusting as needed to be sure they are all the same.
13. Cut a 24" piece of armature wire. Bend into a 5" x 7" rectangle with the beginning and end of the wire at bottom center.
14. Cut an 18" piece of 24 gauge gold wire. Coil around a scrap of armature wire. Remove coil.
15. Apply glue to cut ends of armature wire rectangle. Slip coiled gold wire over ends to join. Let dry.

Assembling the Frame:
16. Arrange s-shapes as shown in photo. Cut a 12" piece of 24 gauge brass wire. Wire two shapes together with wrapped wire (Fig. 3), positioning wrap as shown in photo. Feed beginning of wire through wrap and pull tightly with needle nose pliers. (Fig. 4)
17. Feed end of wire through wrap and pull tightly. (Fig. 5) Trim ends closely.
17. Use wire wraps to join remaining s-shapes, following the same procedure.
18. Use wrapped wire to attach s-shapes to the wire rectangle.
19. Place frame on a flat surface. Press to flatten.
20. Apply glue to back of rectangular part of wire frame. Place wire frame on acrylic frame. Place a large book over frame to hold it while glue dries.
21. Secure acrylic frame to wire frame by running 24 gauge wire through holes in acrylic frame and twisting around armature wire.
22. Attach adhesive hanger to back of acrylic frame. ∽

Wood & Wire

PHOTO FRAME

Pictured on page 89

Designed by Vivian Peritts

◆ SUPPLIES

Wooden frame, 7" x 9" (5" x 7" opening)
14 gauge armature wire, 9'
20 gauge aluminum wire, 15'
9 irregularly shaped pieces clear iridescent stained glass (pieces range in size from approximately 3/4" x 1" to 3/4" x 1-1/4")

◆ TOOLS & EQUIPMENT

Jewelry glue
Wire cutters
Round nose pliers

◆ INSTRUCTIONS

Shaping the wire will be easier if you use Fig. 1 as a pattern.
1. Cut four pieces armature wire to make the four coiled and curved shapes on the frame: 21" (upper left), 25" (lower left), 21" (upper right), and 14" (lower right). Shape pieces according to Fig. 1.
2. Cut nine 18" pieces 20 gauge wire. Wrap glass pieces, using Fig. 2 as a guide. Leave tails on both ends.
3. Arrange armature wire pieces according to Fig. 2. Secure wrapped glass pieces to armature wire, wrapping the wire tails around the armature wire shapes. Tuck ends under.
4. Glue wire shapes to frame according to Fig. 2. ∽

See pages 90 - 91 for Figures 1 and 2.

Wood & Wire

Pictured on page 89

Fig. 1 - Pattern for wire shapes.

Fig. 2 - Guide for placement
of glass pieces.

Gold & Gems

PHOTO FRAME

Designed by Vivian Peritts

♦ **SUPPLIES**

Wooden frames:
   5" x 6" rectangle with 2" x 3" opening
   4-1/2" x 5-3/4" oval with 1-1/2" x
   2-3/4" opening
16 gauge brass wire, 6'
24 gauge copper wire, 10'
4 glass cabochons (1 clear, 1 blue, 1 green,
   1 amber), 3/4"
Rusted metal faux finish paint kit

♦ **TOOLS & EQUIPMENT**

Wire cutters
Needle nose pliers
Jewelry or metal glue

♦ **INSTRUCTIONS**

1. Apply a rusted metal faux paint finish to
   both wooden frames, following kit
   instructions. Let dry.
2. Cut an 8' piece 24 gauge copper wire.
   Wrap oval frame with wire, beginning
   and ending wire on back.
3. Glue oval frame on top of rectangular
   frame.
4. Following pattern, curl and bend 16
   gauge brass wire. Glue wire pieces to
   frame as shown on pattern.
5. Cut four 6" pieces 24 gauge copper wire.
   Wrap each glass cabochon with wire.
   Glue wrapped cabochons to frame. ∽

Pattern for wire design.

Octagon Ornament

FRAMED MIRROR

Designed by Patty Cox

♦ **SUPPLIES**

Octagon mirror with beveled edges, 5"
13 gauge copper wire
22 gauge copper wire
Black felt

♦ **TOOLS & EQUIPMENT**

Needle nose pliers
Jewelry or metal glue

♦ **INSTRUCTIONS**

1. Cut an octagon shape from felt that is slightly smaller than mirror.
2. Cut a piece of 13 gauge wire 16-1/2" long. Form into an octagon shape, following edges of mirror, making the shape 1/16" inside the mirror on all sides. Bend both ends at 90 degree angles. (Fig. 1)
3. Cut four pieces of 13 gauge wire, each 6". Form into triangles. (Fig. 2)
4. Cut eight pieces of 13 gauge wire, each 6-1/2". Form into eight swirls. (Fig. 3)
5. On a flat surface, arrange triangles and swirls around wire octagon. Attach two swirls with wraps of 22 gauge wire. (Fig. 4) Secure and clip ends. Attach swirls to make four pairs.
6. Wrap triangles to octagon shape with 22 gauge wire. (Fig. 5) Secure and clip ends.
7. Wrap pairs of swirls to triangles and wire octagon. (Fig. 5)
8. Form a hanging loop from an 8" piece of 22 gauge wire. Loop around bent ends of wire octagon. Secure and clip ends. (Fig. 6)
9. Apply a generous amount of glue along back edge of mirror. Glue wire octagon to mirror back. Let glue dry. Apply another bead of glue around edges to seal. Let dry.
10. Glue felt to back of mirror. ∾

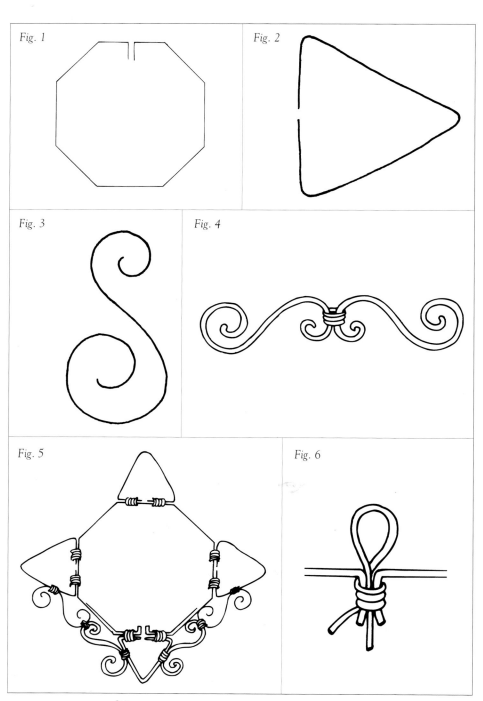

Fig. 1

Fig. 2

Fig. 3

Fig. 4

Fig. 5

Fig. 6

Man in the Moon

FRAMED WIRE ART

Designed by Patty Cox

◆ SUPPLIES

Watercolor paper, 5" x 5"
Watercolor paints:
    Blue
    Violet
16 gauge silver buss wire
24 gauge gold wire
Frame

◆ TOOLS & EQUIPMENT

Artist's paint brush
Needle nose pliers
Cellophane tape
Straight pin

◆ INSTRUCTIONS

1. Cut a piece of silver wire 24" long. Using pattern in Fig. 1 and starting at eye, coil wire around needle nose pliers. Bend wire to shape nose and follow pattern, completing design to overlap wire on forehead.
2. Cut a 6" piece of gold wire. Wrap gold wire around ends of silver wire to secure. Secure ends of gold wire.
3. Using a paint brush, stroke violet, then blue on watercolor paper, using photo as a guide for placement. Let dry.
4. Cut two pieces gold wire, each 1-1/2". Position moon shape on paper. With straight pin, make two tiny holes on either side of silver wire on forehead and below mouth. Loop a piece of gold wire over silver wire and through holes. Twist ends together on back to secure. Cover ends with tape.
5. Place in frame. ⟳

Fig. 1 - Pattern for Moon Shape

Hearts & Spirals

BLOCK PHOTO HOLDER

Designed by Patty Cox

◆ **SUPPLIES**

13 gauge copper wire, 7-1/2'
Wooden cube, 2"
Acrylic craft paint, black
Gloss jewelry glaze
2" square black felt

◆ **TOOLS & EQUIPMENT**

Drill and 1/8" drill bit
Safety goggles or glasses
Household cement
White craft glue
Wooden dowel, 1/2" diameter
Jumbo craft stick
2 thick rubber bands

◆ **INSTRUCTIONS**

Preparing the Cube:

1. Drill five holes 1/2" deep in top of wooden cube. See Fig. 1 for placement. **Always** wear safety glasses or goggles when using a drill.
2. Paint cube with black paint. Let dry.
3. Glue black felt on bottom of cube with white craft glue. Let dry.

Making the Wire Shapes:

4. Cut six pieces copper wire: 21", 19", 17", 15" and 13" (for photo holders) and 5" (for heart on base).
5. To make photo holders, hold one end of one piece of wire with needle nose pliers. Wrap wire to form coil. Form one side of heart shape. Bend bottom point and pinch with needle nose pliers. Form other side of heart. (Fig. 2)
6. Bring wire down 2-3" and wrap wire around dowel three times to form spiral. Leave end of wire straight. Repeat the procedure to make five heart-and-spiral shapes of different lengths.
7. With remaining 5" wire, make the heart for the base. (Fig. 3)

Assembling:

8. Drip a few drops of household cement in each drilled hole on the base. Insert a wire photo holder in each hole. Wipe away excess glue. Let dry.
9. Glue heart to front of base with household cement. Place jumbo craft stick over heart and slip rubber bands over stick. (This will hold the wire heart against the block until the glue dries.) When dry, remove rubber bands and craft stick.
10. Apply a coat of jewelry glaze to base. Let dry. ∽

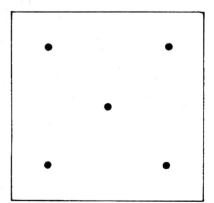

Fig. 1 - Drilling Pattern for Top of Base

Drill 3/8" from corners and at center.

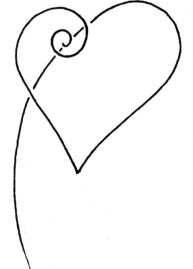

Fig. 2 - Wire Shape for Photo Holders

Fig. 3 - Wire Shape for Base Heart

Wire Works Baskets

Wire is a wonderful material for making woven containers. In this chapter, you'll see a downspout strainer used as a base for a woven wire basket with beads, a fanciful basket shaped from wire mesh, and a pouch made from screening wire to hold potpourri. ∽

Sweet Scents

WIRE POTPOURRI POUCH

Designed by Marion Brizendine

◆ SUPPLIES

Aluminum screen wire
22 gauge copper wire
Handful of pebbles scented with potpourri
   oil
15-20 beads and charms, assorted sizes and
   colors (glass, metal, stone, and resin)—
   your choice
1 round bead, 22 x 4 mm
Brass or copper chain, 14" long

◆ TOOLS & EQUIPMENT

Old scissors or metal shears
Needle nose pliers

◆ INSTRUCTIONS

1. Cut a piece of screen wire 8" x 15".
2. Fold all edges under 3/8". Press flat.
3. Fold one end to make a point. Fold wire to make pouch. (Fig. 1)
4. Loop copper wire over edges of screen on sides to "stitch" sides closed and make pouch, leaving a 1" tail on each end of copper wire. Leave pointed flap of pouch free.
5. Fill pouch with scented pebbles. Fold pointed flap down to close pouch. Attach a bead to the flap with wire to hold the flap closed.
6. Make small curlicues with copper wire. Attach and secure beads and charms. Attach one end of each curlicue to upper fold on pouch. See photo.
7. Attach chain to ends of wire tails on sides to make hanger. ∾

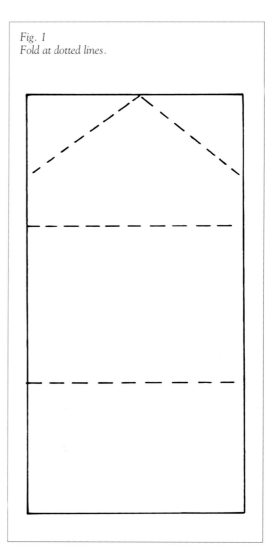

Fig. 1
Fold at dotted lines.

Meshed Gold

WIRE MESH BASKET

Designed by Patty Cox

◆ SUPPLIES

40 gauge bronze wire mesh
20 gauge gold wire
1 diamond-shaped blue glass bead, 16 mm
1 round blue glass bead, 5 mm
1 bronze mushroom bead, 7 mm
1 gold headpin

◆ TOOLS & EQUIPMENT

Old scissors or metal shears
Round nose pliers
Round form, about 3" diameter (a flower
    pot, for example)
Pencil

◆ INSTRUCTIONS

1. Using old scissors or metal shears, cut a 12" square of wire mesh. Fold edges under 1/4". Flatten fold by pressing with scissors handle.
2. Place center of screen over round form. Pleat and fold screen around form.
3. Cut a 36" piece of gold wire. Wrap wire tightly three times around gold mesh about 1-3/4" from bottom to hold shape. Twist ends of gold wire to secure, leaving 3" tails.
4. Wrap tails of wire around a pencil to coil.
5. Thread round bead, then mushroom bead, then diamond-shaped bead on headpin. Loop end of headpin with round nosed pliers. Hook loop over gold wire around basket between coils. Tighten loop of headpin.
6. Shape top of basket, using photo as a guide. ◈

Beaded Weaving

WIRE BASKET

Designed by Patty Cox

◆ SUPPLIES

Downspout strainer to fit a 3" downspout (available at hardware stores and lumber yards)
1 spool 24 gauge silver wire
125 beads, assorted sizes, shapes, and colors (includes round, square, and mushroom shapes; frosted and clear glass and metals), 2mm to 8mm
Metallic gold rub-on wax

◆ TOOLS & EQUIPMENT

Needle nose pliers

◆ INSTRUCTIONS

1. With needle nose pliers, bend the end of each wire of the strainer into a coil to form the upper edge of the basket.
2. Cut 1 yd. 24 gauge wire. Starting at the center bottom, wrap wire five times around one wire rib of the basket to secure the 24 gauge wire. Thread wire over next rib, and wrap wire around rib once. Continue around basket, wrapping the wire around the ribs. Add a bead between the wraps every so often.

TIPS:
- Space the wraps on the basket frame, using photo as a guide.
- When you come to the end of a piece of wire, wrap the end tightly around a rib five times. Pinch with pliers and trim end.
- To start another wire wrap, cut a piece of wire, wrap it around the rib five times, pinch with pliers to secure, and continue to wrap and add beads.

When you get to the top of the basket, wrap end of wire securely and trim end.

3. Apply metallic gold wax to wire part of basket, following package instructions. ๛

Wire Works Candle Holders

Steel baling wire, solder wire, armature wire, and silver buss wire are just some of the options for making and decorating candlesticks and candle holders. Wire also can be used to embellish the candles themselves. ෨

Funky Pair

CANDLESTICKS

These candlesticks are made from ordinary baling wire and accented with wooden beads. Instead of the beads, crystals, old drop earrings, or costume jewelry pendants could be used as accents. Look for old jewelry at yard and tag sales.

Designed by Sonny Knox

◆ SUPPLIES

16 gauge steel baling wire
20 gauge steel bailing wire
Beads:
    2 round gold wooden beads, 1/2"
    2 round white wooden beads, 5/8"
    4 flat hot pink wooden beads, 3/4"
      diameter
    4 flat yellow wooden beads, 3/4" diameter
    4 flat orange wooden beads, 3/4" diameter
    2 round black beads with white dots, 7/8"
    2 domed pink wooden beads, 5/8"
    2 black and white bell-shaped beads,
      5/8" long
Flat black spray paint

◆ TOOLS & EQUIPMENT

Needle nose pliers
Piece of PVC plastic pipe, 3" diameter
Piece of PVC plastic pipe, 4" diameter

◆ INSTRUCTIONS

Cutting the Pieces:
1. Cut two 6" pieces 20 gauge wire.
2. Cut 16 gauge wire to these lengths:
    18 pieces, each 24"
    Two pieces, each 10"
    Two pieces, each 30"
    Two pieces, each 36"
    Four pieces, each 6"

Making the Candle Cup:
These instructions are for making one candlestick. Repeat to make the second candlestick.

Since the wire comes from a roll, all kinks in the wire need to be straightened by hand. This can be tedious, but it is necessary. "Wire" in these instructions refers to 16 gauge wire, unless otherwise noted.

3. Hold eight pieces of 24" wire. With a piece of 6" wire, bind them together 3" from one end. (Fig. 2) The binding wire should be coiled in a tight spiral with no spaces between the loops, much like a compressed spring. (The spring can be fine-tuned with pliers to further compress the spring. Use two pairs of pliers working in opposite directions to tighten the spring.) Nip off any excess.
4. Bend the 3" sections outward like the spokes of a wheel. (Fig. 3)
5. With needle nose pliers, bend each wire back up to form the cup for the candle. The cup should be slightly wider than the base of a candle, and the wires should meet in a point. (Fig. 4)
6. With a 10" piece of wire, form a ring around the base of a candle, keeping the fit snug. (Fig. 5) Circle three times. Nip any excess. Fit the ring over the wires. (Fig. 6) The cup should be about 1" deep.
7. Bend the wires to form the rim around the candle cup. (Fig. 7)
8. With needle nose pliers, curl the ends of the wires. (Fig. 8)

Making the Shaft, Base & Tendrils:
9. Align 30" and 36" wires with the 8 wires at the end opposite the candle cup. Measure 11" from that end and bind with a 6" wire, making a tight spiral coil as described in step 3.
10. Bind the 8-wire shaft at the center with a 6" piece of 20 gauge wire.

continued on page 110

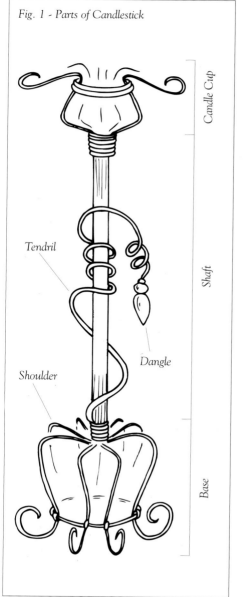

Fig. 1 - Parts of Candlestick

Candle Cup

Tendril

Shaft

Dangle

Shoulder

Base

Funky Pair

CANDLESTICKS

Pictured on page 109

continued from page 108

11. Bend the 11" segments below the bottom binding like the spokes of a wheel, bending the wires up past the 90 degree point. (Fig. 9)
12. Bend the wires back down to form a point. (Fig. 10) The width of the shoulder of the base should be about 4". *Optional:* Use a piece of 4" PVC pipe to aid in bending the wire.
13. Using a 3" piece of PVC pipe as a form, bend a 24" piece of wire into a circle. Go around the circle two times and firmly twist the ends to secure. Fit the circle over the point of the wires and position it about 2-1/2" below the shoulder of the base. (Fig. 11)
14. Bend each wire out and around the circle to secure each leg to the wire ring, using needle nose pliers to tighten the wires. (Fig. 12) Work on opposite wires, keeping the ring level.
15. Using needle nose pliers, roll all legs into graceful spirals right up to the lower ring. (Fig. 13) Adjust as needed so the candlestick stands up straight.

Forming the Tendrils & Dangles:

16. At the end of each of the two tendrils, make a small loop, using needle nose pliers. Holding the loop at the tip with the pliers, wrap the wire around the pliers to form a spiral. (Fig. 14) (A little loosening may be necessary to release the pliers.)
17. Stand the candlestick on its feet and arrange the tendrils around the shaft. (Fig. 1 and photo) Add curves and corkscrew shaping, being sure the ends point down.
18. Make the dangles from 10" pieces of wire. Make a corkscrew shape around needle nose pliers, but don't make a loop on the end. Straighten the other end.

continued on next page

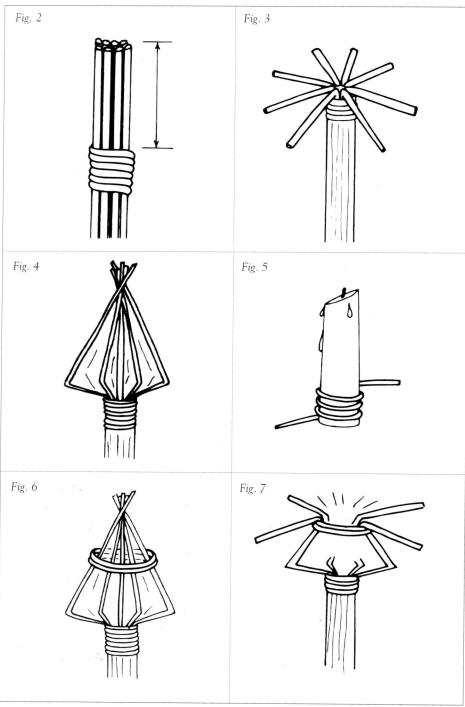

Fig. 2

Fig. 3

Fig. 4

Fig. 5

Fig. 6

Fig. 7

continued from page 110

Finishing & Assembly:

19. Spray candlestick and dangles with black spray paint. Let dry completely.
20. Thread beads on the dangles, using photo as a guide. (The corkscrew shape will hold them on the wire.) Make a loop at the end and attach to the end of the tendril. Repeat to complete remaining dangles and attach. ∽

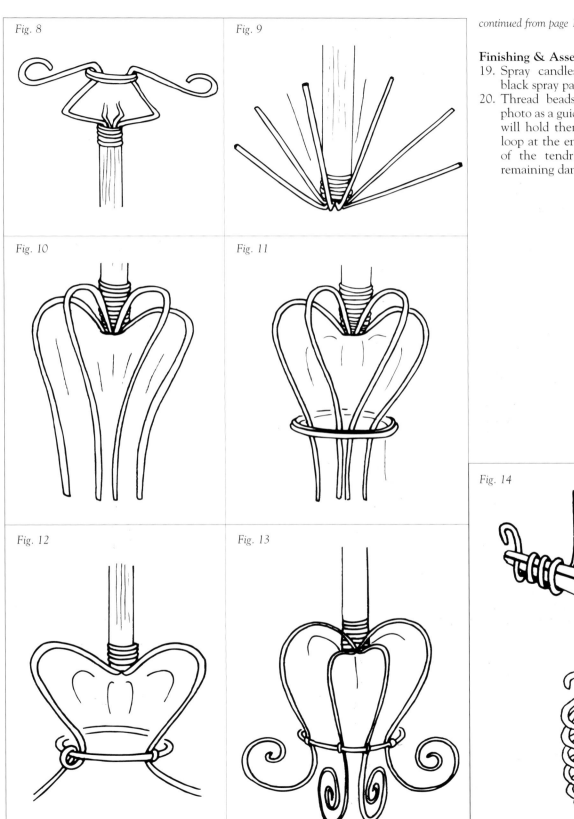

Fig. 8

Fig. 9

Fig. 10

Fig. 11

Fig. 12

Fig. 13

Fig. 14

Pliers

Spirals & Beads

CANDLE HOLDER

Designed by Sonny Knox

♦ **SUPPLIES**

16 gauge steel baling wire
20 gauge steel bailing wire
1 pink wooden bead, 1"
1 blue wooden bead, 3/4"
1 red wooden bead, 3/4"
1 yellow wooden bead, 1/2"
Flat black spray paint

♦ **TOOLS & EQUIPMENT**

Needle nose pliers
Piece of PVC plastic pipe, 3" diameter
Piece of PVC plastic pipe, 4" diameter

♦ **INSTRUCTIONS**

Cutting the Pieces:
1. Cut one 6" piece 20 gauge wire.
2. Cut 16 gauge wire to these lengths:
   9 pieces, each 24"
   Three pieces, each 10"
   One piece, 30"
   One piece, 12"
   One piece, 18"
   Three pieces, 6"

Making the Candle Cup:
Since the wire comes from a roll, all kinks in the wire need to be straightened by hand before forming the candlestick. This can be tedious, but it is necessary. "Wire" in these instructions refers to 16 gauge wire, unless otherwise noted.
3. Follow steps 3 - 8 of the previous project, "Funky Pair," to form the candle cup.

continued on page 114

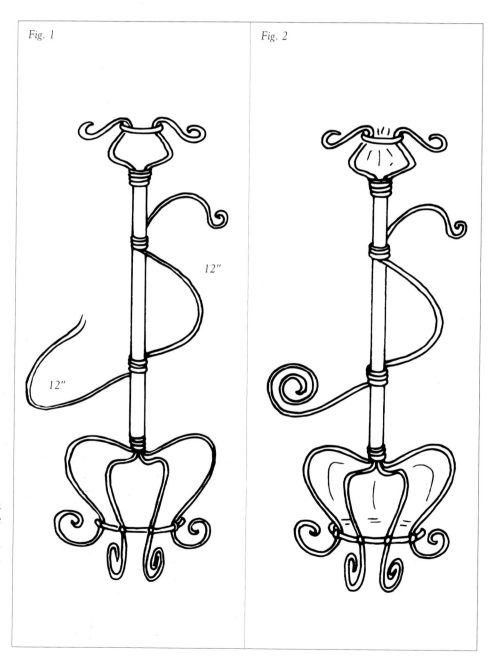

Fig. 1

12"

12"

Fig. 2

Spirals & Beads

CANDLE HOLDER

Pictured on page 113

continued from page 112

Making the Base:
4. Measure 11" from the opposite end and bind with a 6" wire, making a tight spiral coil as described in step 3 of "Funky Pair."
5. Follow steps 11 - 15 of the previous project, "Funky Pair," to form the base.

Making the Spirals & Finishing:
6. Measure to find the midpoint of the 30" piece. Attach the center to the shaft about 3" above the base, wrapping the wire around the shaft tightly. Leave 12" below the wrapping and 12" above it. (Fig. 1)
7. Make an s-curve on the upper end and loop the end. Attach by wrapping with 20 gauge wire about 4" up the shaft. (Fig. 1)
8. Spray candlestick and three remaining wire pieces with black paint. Let dry completely.
9. Add the red bead to the wire on the left side of the candle. Form a tight hook at the end to anchor the bead and roll the wire into a spiral. (Fig. 2)
10. Make additional spirals with beads, using the pink bead with the 18" wire, the blue bead with the 12" wire, and the yellow bead with the 6" wire. Use the last 3/4" of each piece to form a hook to attach the spirals. (Fig. 3)
11. Join the spirals and hang from the hook on the right. Adjust to balance. ∾

Fig. 3

Silver Coils

VOTIVE HOLDER

Designed by Patty Cox

◆ SUPPLIES

Clear round glass votive holder
Aluminum armature wire, 14 gauge

◆ TOOLS & EQUIPMENT

Needle nose pliers
Jewelry or metal glue

◆ INSTRUCTIONS

1. Cut four 10" pieces aluminum wire. Hold end of one piece with needle nose pliers and coil wire. Repeat to form four slightly irregular small coils.
2. Cut four 16" pieces aluminum wire. Hold end of one piece with needle nose pliers and coil wire. Repeat to form four slightly irregular large coils.
3. Glue coils on sides of votive holder, alternating large and small coils. ∾

Wires & Baubles

CANDLE & HOLDER

Designed by Vivian Peritts

◆ SUPPLIES

Ivory pillar candle, 8" tall, 2-1/2" diameter
Clear glass candle holder, 4" tall, 4" wide
16 glass cabochons, 3/4", in various colors
14 gauge aluminum armature wire, 28'
White wax, enough to fill a tall container
   (See step 4, below)

◆ TOOLS & EQUIPMENT

Wire cutters
Needle nose pliers
Jewelry or metal glue
Terry cloth towel
1 qt. glass and mirror etching liquid
Plastic container slightly wider and twice
   as tall as candle holder, to hold the
   etching liquid
Tall metal container, as tall as the candle
   and slightly wider, for dipping the can-
   dle in melted wax
Double boiler
Permanent marker or masking tape
Wax paper

See pages 118 & 119 for Figs. 1 and 2.

◆ INSTRUCTIONS

Decorating the Candle:

1. Using shapes of Fig. 1 as a guide, shape wires with needle nose pliers.
2. Use your hand to mold the wire pieces to the round shape of the candle.
3. Place the towel on a work surface. Place the candle on its side on the towel, so the candle won't roll. Glue the shaped wires and nine of the cabochons on the candle. Glue one section at a time. Let dry completely before turning the candle and gluing the next section. Let dry 24 hours.
4. To estimate how much wax will be needed, place the candle in the tall container. Add enough water to cover the candle. Remove the candle and mark the water level with a permanent marker or a piece of tape. Pour the water in the top of the double boiler. Note how full the top of the double boiler is. Pour out the water. Dry the tall container and the top of the double boiler.
5. Pour water in the bottom of the double boiler. Place the wax in the top of the dou- ble boiler. Place double boiler on stove. Melt wax, adding wax until you have enough to fill the tall container to the mark. Take the double boiler off the stove. Carefully pour the wax into the tall container until the wax reaches the mark.
6. Holding the candle wick with the pliers, dip the candle in the wax. Remove candle and place on a piece of wax paper for three minutes. Dip candle again. Remove. Wait three minutes. Dip again. Remove. Let dry.

Decorating the Candle Holder:

7. Place the candle holder in the plastic container. Pour in enough water to complete- ly cover the candle holder. Remove the candle holder. Mark the water level on the outside of the container with a permanent marker or a piece of tape. Pour out the water. Dry the container.
8. Pour etching liquid in the plastic container up to the mark. Following package instructions for etching glass, place candle holder and seven cabochons in the liquid. Leave in the liquid as long as directed.
9. Remove candle holder and cabochons from liquid and rinse in water as directed. Let dry.
10. Cut three pieces of 14 gauge wire, each 40" long. Make a coil at the end of each wire with needle nose pliers by coiling and bending from the end of each wire. See Fig. 2 for ideas.
11. Wrap the center of each piece of wire, one at a time, around the neck of the candle holder. Gently curve the design area to conform to the shape of the candle holder.
12. Glue the cabochons to the wire randomly, using photo as a guide for placement. ∾

Wire & Baubles

CANDLE & HOLDER

Pictured on page 117

Fig. 1 - Wire shapes for Candle

Fig. 2 - Suggested wire shapes for Candle Holder

7"

7"

23"

23"

10"

10"

Wire Cone

CANDLE HOLDER

Designed by Sonny Knox

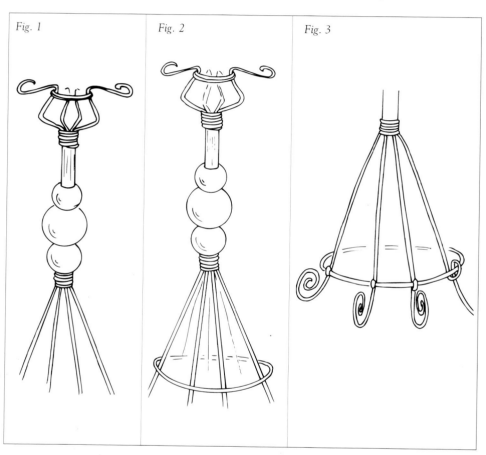

Fig. 1

Fig. 2

Fig. 3

◆ SUPPLIES

16 gauge steel baling wire
20 gauge steel bailing wire
2 large-bore green wooden beads, 7/8"
1 large-bore yellow wooden bead, 1-1/4"
Flat black spray paint

◆ TOOLS & EQUIPMENT

Needle nose pliers
Piece of PVC plastic pipe, 4" diameter

◆ INSTRUCTIONS

Cutting the Pieces:
1. Cut 16 gauge wire to these lengths:
   8 pieces, each 24"
   Two pieces, each 10"
   One piece, 36"
   Two pieces, 6"

Making the Candle Cup:
Since the wire comes from a roll, all kinks in the wire need to be straightened by hand before forming the candlestick. This can be tedious, but it is necessary.
2. Follow steps 3 - 8 of the project "Funky Pair" to form the candle cup.
3. Spray the candlestick and remaining pieces of wire with black paint. Let dry.

Making the Base:
4. Add the beads to the shaft from the unfinished end. See photo for placement. Wrap the shaft below the beads, 4" below the candle cup, with a 10" piece of wire, making a spiral coil. Double wrap the wire at the top to hold the beads on the shaft. (Fig. 1)

5. Take the long wires and splay them outward gently. (Fig. 2)
6. With the 36" piece of wire, form a lower ring 4" in diameter. Secure ends with a firm twist.
7. Fit the ring over the lower ends of the wires 5-6" above the ends of the wires.
8. Bend each wire out and around the circle to secure each leg to the wire ring, using needle nose pliers to tighten the wires. (Fig. 3) Work on opposite wires, keeping the ring level.
9. Using needle nose pliers, roll all legs into graceful spirals right up to the lower ring. (Fig. 3) Adjust as needed so the candlestick stands up straight.
10. Touch up paint, if needed. Be sure to shield beads from the paint. Let dry. ∾

Woven Wire

CANDLE JAR

Designed by Beth Cosner

◆ SUPPLIES

Clear glass pillar candle holder, 6" tall, 5" diameter at bottom with flared top
18 gauge copper wire, 16-1/2'
Half-round brass wire, 30"
4 round wooden balls with one flattened side, 1-1/2" diameter (sold as dolls' heads)
4 (2 teal, 2 red) teardrop shaped glass beads, 1" long
2 teal glass beads, 4 x 8 mm
2 clear glass beads with red swirls, 10 x 15 mm
Acrylic craft paint, copper metallic
Clear sealer spray

◆ TOOLS & EQUIPMENT

Small paint brush
Jewelry glue
Drill or drilling tool
Gloves
Face shield or safety goggles
Wire cutters
Round nose pliers
Flat nose pliers
Jeweler's tweezers
1/16" drill bit for wood
1/16" drill bit for cutting glass (solid carbide bit or glass and tile bit)

◆ INSTRUCTIONS

Making the Wooden Feet:
1. Place the wooden balls so the flattened side is on the bottom. Drill a hole 1/16" dia. x 1/2" deep at the center top of each.
2. Paint with copper paint. Let dry. Paint with a second coat. Let dry.
3. Spray with clear sealer. Set aside.

Wrapping the Copper Wire:
4. Drill two holes 1/16" dia. in the glass pillar holder, using a drill bit for glass. Align the two holes vertically, placing one about 1" down from the top edge and the other 1" up from the bottom. Wear safety goggles and gloves when drilling glass.
5. Wash the glass pillar holder in warm, soapy water. Dry or let dry.
6. Working from the outside in, thread about 1" of copper wire through lower hole in glass. Attach one small teal bead (not a teardrop shaped one) on the wire inside the glass. Trim end of wire and, using needle nose pliers, make a small loop to hold the bead on the wire.
7. Thread a clear bead with a red swirl down the length of the copper wire. Pass wire around bead and twist behind bead to secure and hold bead flat against glass in front of hole.
8. Wrap the copper wire around the glass candle holder 11 times, spacing the wraps fairly evenly. Stop when you reach the hole near the top. **Do not** wrap the wire tightly—remember that the brass wire will be woven through the copper.
9. Thread a clear bead with a red swirl on the copper wire. Pass wire around bead and twist behind bead to secure and hold bead flat against glass in front of hole.
10. Thread tail of wire through hole and pass through remaining small teal bead. Secure bead **lightly**. **Do not** cut off end of wire.

Weaving the Brass Wire:
11. Cut four pieces brass half-round wire, each 7-1/2". Weave the brass wire vertically through the copper wire, going under and over the copper. Let 1" extend above the candle holder and 1/2" extend below the candle holder. Repeat with remaining three pieces of brass, spacing them evenly around the candle holder.
- As you add the third and fourth brass pieces, the weaving will become more difficult because there will be less slack in the copper wire. It may be necessary to create a bit more slack in the copper wire by loosening the beads.
- Jeweler's tweezers are useful for moving the wires when weaving.

Finishing:
12. Cut off excess copper wire, leaving enough to make a loop to secure the teal bead at the inside top.
13. Insert brass wires at bottom of candle holder in holes drilled in wooden balls. Secure with glue.
14. Glue teardrop shaped beads on top ends of brass wire, alternating colors. ✑

Decorated Bright

CANDLE ORNAMENT & HOLDER

Designed by Patty Cox

◆ SUPPLIES

Silver armature wire
22 gauge silver wire
16 gauge silver buss wire
3 prisms with gold caps, 1" long
3 jump rings
Round candle

◆ TOOLS & EQUIPMENT

Needle nose pliers
For the template:
1/4" diameter dowel, 8" long
Saw
6" piece of 2 x 4 lumber
Drill and 1/4" bit
Tracing paper
Transfer paper and stylus

◆ INSTRUCTIONS

Making the Template:
1. Trace pattern for template. (Fig. 1) Transfer pattern to 2 x 4 wood.
2. Drill holes 3/8" deep in 2 x 4 wood.
3. Cut dowel in pieces 1" long. Insert dowel pieces in holes.

Making the Candle Ornament:
4. Cut an 18" piece of 16 gauge wire. Fold wire around top center dowel. Pull wires to center, criss cross wire, and wrap around two lower center dowels. End at dowels on either end. (Fig. 1) Lift wire from template.
5. Bend the last 3/16" of each end of the wire at a 90 degree angle. (Fig. 2) Position ornament on candle and press bent ends into candle.

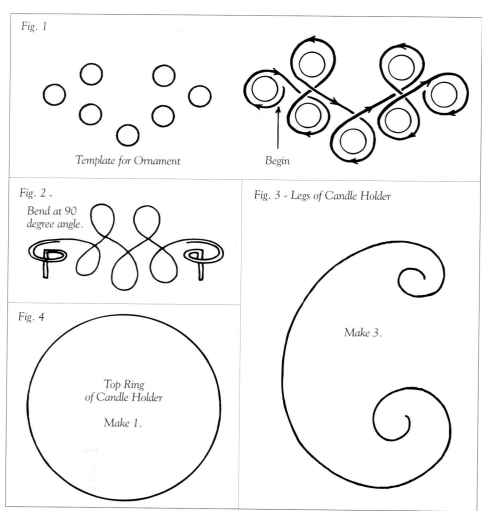

Fig. 1

Template for Ornament　　*Begin*

Fig. 2
Bend at 90 degree angle.

Fig. 3 - Legs of Candle Holder

Make 3.

Fig. 4

*Top Ring
of Candle Holder*

Make 1.

Making the Candle Holder:
6. Make three curved c-shapes from armature wire. (Fig. 3)
7. Form a ring from armature wire 2" in diameter. (Fig. 4)
8. Wrap three c-shapes together at center with 22 gauge wire. Secure and clip ends.
9. Position c-shapes to form a tripod. Place ring on top of tripod. Wrap ring to tripod with 22 gauge wire. Secure and clip ends.
10. Attach prisms to top ring with jump rings. ∞

Simplicity

GLASS CANDLESTICK

Designed by Marion Brizendine

◆ **SUPPLIES**

Clear glass candlestick, 10" tall
Silver solid lead free solder, .081 gauge
4 green pony beads, 6 mm
3 white pony beads, 6 mm

◆ **TOOLS & EQUIPMENT**

Needle nose pliers
Jewelry or metal glue

◆ **INSTRUCTIONS**

1. Make a tight coil of wire 1/2" in diameter. Hold coil on base of candlestick with thumb of one hand.
2. With other hand, wrap wire around shaft of candlestick, adding beads here and there, ending the wrap around the bottom of the candle holder at top. Cut off excess wire, leaving enough to make a coil 3/8" in diameter.
3. Glue coils to base and candle holder as shown in photo. ⁀

Metric Conversion Chart

Inches to Millimeters and Centimeters

Inches	MM	CM
1/8	3	.3
1/4	6	.6
3/8	10	1.0
1/2	13	1.3
5/8	16	1.6
3/4	19	1.9
7/8	22	2.2
1	25	2.5
1-1/4	32	3.2
1-1/2	38	3.8
1-3/4	44	4.4
2	51	5.1
3	76	7.6
4	102	10.2
5	127	12.7
6	152	15.2
7	178	17.8
8	203	20.3
9	229	22.9
10	254	25.4
11	279	27.9
12	305	30.5

Yards to Meters

Yards	Meters
1/8	.11
1/4	.23
3/8	.34
1/2	.46
5/8	.57
3/4	.69
7/8	.80
1	.91
2	1.83
3	2.74
4	3.66
5	4.57
6	5.49
7	6.40
8	7.32
9	8.23
10	9.14

Index

Acrylic paint (see paint)
Aluminum wire 8,
Armature wire 8, 9

Bailing wire108, 112, 120
Baskets 100-105
Beaded Weaving 105
Beads 11, 16, 18, 20, 24, 28, 31, 32, 34, 46,
    58, 60, 69, 74, 76, 78, 102, 104, 105, 108,
    112, 120, 122, 126
Beads & Glamour 60
Bolt 13
Bottle 46, 48
Bottles & Vases 44-51
Bracelet 22, 25, 31, 32
Buss wire 8, 9

Cabochons 11, 22, 46, 48, 50, 54, 56, 66, 69,
    76, 84, 92, 116
Candle Holders 106-126
Choker 20
Circles & Gems 50
Circles & Stones 69
Clasps 11
Clay pot 62, 64
Cobalt & Copper 31
Coils & Twists 26
Copper Cat 36
Copper Coils 22
Copper Swirls 30
Cotter pins 12, 25, 26
Cutters 10, 25, 26, 32, 46, 48, 60, 66, 72, 74,
    88, 92, 102, 104, 116, 122

Dangling Star 38
Dappled with Gold 32Deco Diamonds 66
Decorated Bright 124
Dowels 10, 30, 32, 98, 124
Downspout strainer 78, 105
Drill 74, 98, 122, 124

Earring backs 11
Earrings 16, 18, 20, 22, 26, 30, 31
Epoxy (see Glue)
Etching liquid 116
Eyepins 11, 76

Fender washer 12, 13, 25, 26
Figure Eights 30
Findings (see Jewelry findings)
Flatware 54
Flower Garden 62
Frames 80-99
Funky Pair 108

Gloves 11
Glue 10, 22, 24, 25, 26, 37, 46, 48, 50, 54, 56,
    58, 62, 66, 68, 72, 74, 76, 78, 82, 84, 86,
    88, 92, 94, 98, 115, 116, 122, 126
Goblets 60
Goggles 11
Gold & Gems 92
Gold Spirals & Green Beads 18
Golden Mesh Bow 68
Golden Wrapping 25

Head pins 11
Hearts & Spirals 98
Household cement (see Glue)

Jewelry 14-43
Jewelry findings 11, 16, 18, 22, 25, 26, 28, 30,
    31, 32, 37, 40, 42, 43, 124
Jewelry glue (see Glue)
Jump rings 11

Lampshades 70-79

Magenta & Swirls 46
Man in the Moon 96
Mardi Gras 31
Mesh, wire 8, 9, 68, 76, 104
Meshed Gold 104
Metal glue (see Glue)
Mirror 94
Mother of Pearl Nuggets 20

Nail clippers 18, 20
Nails 10, 38, 40, 86
Napkin rings 54, 68
Necklace 16, 18, 24, 28
Nut 13

Oak Leaf 42
Octagon Ornament 94

Paint 37, 48, 62, 82, 84, 96, 98, 108, 112, 120,
    122
Pair of Partners 56
Pearl nuggets 20
Pencil 104
Pendant 38, 42
Pin 26, 34, 36, 37, 40, 42, 43
Pin backs 11
Place Card Favors 62
Plaster 62, 64
Pliers 10, 13, 16, 18, 20, 22, 24, 25, 28, 30, 32,
    34, 37, 38, 40, 42, 43, 46, 48, 54, 56, 62,
    64, 66, 69, 72, 74, 76, 78, 82, 84, 86, 88,
    92, 94, 96, 102, 104, 105, 108, 112, 115,
    116, 120, 122, 124, 126

Plump Pears 42
Pouch 102
Protective gear 11, 74, 122

Red & Silver 28
Rhinestones 37
Rubber bands 58, 98
Rubber cement 82

Salt &Pepper shakers 56
Sapphire Frost 48
Scissors 10, 24
Shades of Art 72
Shaker 58
Shoes with Style 43
Silver Butterfly 37
Silver Coils 115
Silver & Copper Cat 36
Silver Heart 38
Silver Spider 34
Simplicity 126
Solder wire 8, 9
Spirals & Beads 112
Spirals & Curves 54
Stained glass 72, 88
Stones 11
Stones & Swirls 84
Suede & Spirals 82
Sugar & Spice 58
Sweet Rose 37
Sweet Scents 102

Tabletop Glamour 52-69
Thin gauge wire 8, 9
Toothpicks 50, 76, 78
Touch of the West 74
Tracing paper 10, 30, 38, 40, 42, 43, 86, 124
Transfer paper 10, 30, 37, 38, 40, 42, 43, 86,
    124

Vase 50
Victorian Swirls 86

Watering Can 40
Wire Cone 120
Wire & Mesh 76
Wire mesh (see Mesh)
Wire Twists 25
Wires & Baubles 116
Wood & Wire 88
Woven Basket 24
Woven Shade 78
Woven Wire 122
Wrapped Amber 16